THE TALK ABOUT
"THE REMNANT"

This book is very insightful and deals with questions and concerns that are on the hearts of God's people. The Holy Spirit wants to encourage the readers and let them know that no matter what they go through, God has a Remnant of Believers that are living for Him. Renee's experiences show us that God is watching out for His people. I am so excited for her.

~ **Dixie Gardner**

Have you ever wondered what was ahead of the curve in the road you were traveling? Renee shares the lessons learned on her journey, providing scriptural insight with words of encouragement, to prepare one to navigate the unknown. Her authenticity provides a real look at how God comes alongside to direct our steps and illuminate our paths so we can continue to our destiny, even through stormy weather.

~ **Dr. David Dyson, Oral Roberts University, Business Professor, Tulsa, Oklahoma**

i

We live in a world where many have wandered from *the truth*. There still remains a standard that God has called His people to live by and nothing less than conformity to His Word is acceptable. Author Renee Gardner not only reminds us of this standard but she provides a path to get back on it for those who have gone astray. Brilliantly written and wonderfully refreshing, *The Remnant* is a must-read if you are ready to regain your identity, claim your platform, and advance God's Kingdom on Earth!

~ **Dr. Kisia L. Coleman,** M.O.D.E.L. (Mentoring Our Daughters, Equipping Ladies) Ministries, Founder, Kingdom Church Int'l., Co-Founder, KishKnows, Inc., Book Publishing Coach & Self-Publishing Servicer, Chicago, IL

The
REMNANT

An Inspirational Devotional
for Emerging Leaders

RENEE GARDNER

KishKnows
PUBLISHING

The Remnant: An Inspirational Devotional
for Emerging Leaders
by Renee Gardner

Cover design, editing, book layout and publishing services by KishKnows, Inc., Richton Park, Illinois, 708-252-DOIT
admin@kishknows.com, www.kishknows.com

ISBN 978-0-692-09967-4
LCCN 2018903977

Some Scripture references may be paraphrased versions or illustrative references of the author. Unless otherwise indicated, all Scripture quotations are taken from THE HOLY BIBLE, NEW INTERNATIONAL VERSION®, NIV® Copyright © 1973, 1978, 1984, 2011 by Biblica, Inc.® Used by permission. All rights reserved worldwide.

All other Scripture references are taken from the following versions of the Bible and will be referenced as their abbreviations in this book:

NEW AMERICAN STANDARD BIBLE® (NASB) Copyright © 1960, 1962, 1963, 1968, 1971, 1972, 1973, 1975, 1977, 1995 by The Lockman Foundation. Used by permission.

CONTENTS

A NOTE FROM THE AUTHOR

This book is dedicated to those of you starting out on your journey to destiny. You are a part of God's remnant that He is raising up in this generation. I feel a sense of responsibility to share all the things that the Lord has taught me, and is still teaching me, along the journey and share it with others. When much is given, much is required of you.

You may be asking yourself, "What is a remnant? And why is God choosing me?" Merriam-Webster's definition of the word "remnant" is, "*A usually small part, member, or trace remaining.*" This is referring to you and me. We are ambassadors of the Kingdom of God and His representation in the earth for this time and in this generation. In a day and age where God is not considered popular or relevant, God is strategically positioning His Remnant and causing us to have influence for His purposes. God is choosing *you* because His Kingdom purpose must be established throughout the earth. As explained by many Biblical scholars, on several occasions in the Bible you will see times when the children of Israel (God's chosen people) did not follow and obey His commandments. They did not follow God's way all the time, but there were always a faithful few that did not bend to the pressure and stayed true to God's commands and ways of doing things. That group was the remnant.

In Romans 11:1-6, we read the following: "I ask then: Did God reject his people? By no means! I am an Israelite myself, a descendant of Abraham, from the tribe of Benjamin. God did not reject his people, whom he foreknew. Don't you know what Scripture says in the passage about Elijah — how he appealed to God against Israel: 'Lord, they have killed your prophets and torn down your altars; I am the only one left, and they are trying to kill me.' And what was God's answer to him? 'I have reserved for myself seven thousand who have not bowed their knee to Baal so too, at the present time there is a remnant chosen by grace. And if by grace, then it cannot be based on works; if it were, grace would no longer be grace."

God has chosen you by His grace to follow Him — He has chosen you to be part of His Remnant. So, enjoy the journey and trust the Holy Spirit to guide you and to counsel you every step of the way, because you never know where God is taking you

— somewhere great, of course. You have a work to do and this book is for you. God has called you to do a great work. He has chosen *you*.

**"But you are a chosen people, a
royal priesthood, a holy nation,
God's special possession,
that you may declare the praises of him
who called you out of darkness
into his wonderful light."
(1 Peter 2:9)**

DEVOTION 1

Sacrificing for Great Gain

"But what things were gain to me,
these I have counted loss for Christ.
Yet indeed I also count all things loss
for the excellence of the knowledge
of Christ Jesus my Lord,
for whom I have suffered the loss of all things,
and count them as rubbish,
that I may gain Christ."
(Philippians 3:7-8, NKJV)

Have you ever been in a place where you felt as if you were saying no to all the things your flesh wanted — yet, you didn't see anything good come from denying yourself in the natural? I have. You may think that those sacrifices have gone unnoticed, but the Bible says that God keeps a record of our deeds and He remembers when we do good things. Since that is the case, there is a universal law of seedtime and harvest, and when you sow good seeds, you'll reap a good harvest in God's timing. You're not going to be able to do

1

what everyone else is doing all the time. However, a word of encouragement to you is this: Think about all the things you're going to gain because of your choice to say no to your flesh and yes to God.

I remember, back in my college years, most of my friends wanted to go and hang out on the weekends. We would spend time together, watch movies, or go to concerts. However, there was one particular weekend I needed to set aside because I had a big test coming up in my American History class and I was stressing about it. I had to tell my friends, "No, I can't hang out this weekend because I have a big test on Monday, and I am not taking this class over again." This was truly a sacrifice for me because I loved hanging out with my friends but I needed to learn balance, discipline, and responsibility in this season of my life. After studying and working hard, I remember receiving a "B plus" on my test.

Fast forward into my young adult years beyond college. I remember that there was a particular season of my life where opportunities were coming my way left and right. I began to feel overwhelmed and excited at the same time because there were new opportunities such as relocating, relationships, and a new career right in front of me.

Now, the key is to know what opportunity to take and when to take it. All opportunities are not God-opportunities, and we must definitely have discernment and know when to move when God says, "*Move.*"

During this season of my life, I received several job offers that I declined because I did not have peace on the inside. These job offers were in very nice locations and, on the surface, they looked great but there was something inside my spirit that was not at peace with me regarding taking these jobs.

After declining those jobs, another opportunity appeared and I was very interested in accepting a job in California. Now, during this time, I was very careful and went to the Lord in prayer. I didn't want to make any hasty decisions without seeking the counsel of the Lord. I took some time to think things over concerning the job offer and what I should do. If you don't think that God speaks, you have been misinformed — He definitely speaks and He knows just how to get through to you. Later that week, I went to church and felt an unusual move of the Holy Spirit in the service that day. My pastor began to speak prophetically and said, "There are several of you in here contemplating on relocating and accepting business deals and offers, but there are things under the table that you don't know about." He went on to say, "The people that you are dealing with are not disclosing everything to you. There are things under the rug; things left unsaid. They want to use you as a scapegoat and the devil wants to take you somewhere far away to isolate you." This was spot on, and I hadn't even talked to my pastor about this, let alone anyone in the church. The last thing he said was, "A lot of you will have to make some decisions this week."

The very next day, I received a phone call about that particular position and after they had completed my background check, they extended a firm offer of employment to me and needed my final decision on whether I would accept the job. I respectfully declined and thanked them for the opportunity to interview for the job.

Let me tell you that God is several steps ahead of the enemy, and He knows the traps, setups, and plans that the enemy has set in place for you, but He will always reveal the plans of the enemy and provide a way of escape. Please remember that every opportunity is not a God-opportunity, and you want to always seek the Lord on the best decision to take.

Sometimes, we don't want to wait for His answer and trust me, I get it. I've definitely been there and wanted to step out on what I felt in that moment but, remember that your steps are ordered by the Lord, and we should move when God gives us orders to make the next move in life.

Also, in my journey, I've learned that when making big decisions, God is not going to confuse you. He is always on time when He provides an answer and His voice will be so clear for your specific situation and He'll give you the best counsel. Looking back at my situation, I can see how He has been faithful to me and has always been on time. He knows exactly where you are supposed to be. I thank God for the pastors and men and women of God who follow the winds of the Holy Spirit and yield to the voice of God.

**"Since we live by the Spirit,
let us keep in step with the Spirit.
(Galatians 5:25)**

Treasures of Truth

Are there multiple choices in front of you? Do you have to make a decision? If so, make sure that you are in the presence of God and seeking the Lord's counsel. In Psalms 16:11, it says,

**"You will show me the Path of Life;
In your presence is the fullness of joy;
At your right hand are
pleasures forevermore."**

The answers are all found in His Presence. I pray that you take this opportunity to spend time with the Father and seek His counsel and wisdom in order to make the best choice. He already has the blueprint for your life; He designed the plan and knows it in great detail.

Today I Will...

- Spend time with my Heavenly Father and dwell in His Presence.
- Commit my ways to the Lord and seek His face to lead and guide me.
- Know that His timing is perfect.

Let's Pray...

Heavenly Father, please help me to be still and know that you are God. I ask for Your guidance and wisdom to discern what is from You and what is not. Guide me with Your mighty hand in the right direction.

In Jesus' Name,

Amen.

DEVOTION 2

I Can See Clearly Now

**"He lifted me out of the pit of despair,
out of the mud and the mire.
He set my feet on solid ground
and steadied me as I walked along."
(Psalm 40:2, NLT)**

Do you feel like you are in a pit, stuck, or feel powerless? I can relate. I remember lying in bed one night; thinking about the past choices and passed over opportunities that I had let go of in my past. I began to think about the "what ifs." If I had chosen differently, how better would my life have been?

At that moment, I thought to myself, "Renee, you waited too late. It's too late. So many people are so far beyond you." I continued to beat myself up inside and literally cried myself to sleep. At that moment, I had allowed the cares of the world to cloud my thinking, and I lost sight of God and the endless opportunities He had for me!

9

Then God woke me up at 1:37am. And I heard God say, *"Just because you waited, it does not change My ability — it does not limit Me, declares the Lord!"* I felt the Sovereignty of God and He reminded me that He is in control and not me! He knows where every provision is and every good break. It was in that pit that I heard God's voice as loud as ever and He reminded me that He's in control. All of my worries and cares ceased at that moment.

If you are going through a time of feeling as if you are in a pit of despair or depression, know that He is sovereign over that pit. Wait until you come out on the other side of this season! There is so much in store for you.

"Instead of your shame you will receive a double portion, and instead of disgrace you will rejoice in your inheritance. And so you will inherit a double portion in your land, and everlasting joy will be yours."
(Isaiah 61:7)

Treasures of Truth

Realize that Christ's love is greater than your pit or any situation that feels or seems stagnant. Remember that God is El Elyon, "The Most High God" and He is the highest. That means, He is higher than any situation or anything that we may face. After all is said and done, you will come out as pure gold. Promotion, favor, success, and blessings are your portion and are waiting for you on the other side of this pit.

We serve an awesome God! No need to worry or fret! No need to compare your life to others and think, "Oh, woe is me!" No way! We have the God of the universe on our side — who can do ANYTHING!!!

**Jesus looked at them intently and said,
"Humanly speaking, it is impossible.
But with God everything is possible."
(Matthew 19:26, NLT)**

Today I Will...

- Run to God when my heart feels overwhelmed.
- Remember that no matter what — God is in control.
- Thank Him for keeping His hand on my life and keep serving Him in all that I do.

Let's Pray...

Most High God, thank you for dispelling every lie of the enemy and bringing hope when things seemed so dark in my life. You are the God of Hope, fill me with all joy and peace in believing that I may abound in hope.

In Jesus' Name,

Amen.

DEVOTION 3

Kingdom Alliances

"'Entreat me not to leave you, Or to turn back from following after you; For wherever you go, I will go; And wherever you lodge, I will lodge; Your people shall be my people, And your God, my God. Where you die, I will die, And there will I be buried. The LORD do so to me, and more also, If *anything* but death parts you and me.'"
(Ruth 1:16-17)

Earlier in my career, when I started my internship and entered into Corporate America in the business field, God started to elevate me in this role. He assigned a prophet to me, and his name was Gabriel — just like the angel.

Now, to the average person, he may have been just a janitor; but to me, he was much more than that. He was the first person that confirmed to me that God had a calling on my life to be a prophetess. He shared some personal things with me about

13

myself, which I had not shared with him or anyone, and the things that he said were true. God used him to prophesy to me about my future, and what he prophesied actually happened.

At the time, I didn't know that God had called me to the prophetic, but the Lord began to show me and He confirmed it three times, via three different people. Gabriel was the first of those people. I remember Gabriel telling me that God had shown him that He had a great work for me to do. Gabriel would come by my desk at the right time, always when I needed an encouraging word. He reassured me that God was hearing my prayers and that He hadn't forgotten about me. He constantly encouraged me to study the Word of God and I felt that God used him to help give me a push to keep going in those times when I wanted to quit. Let me tell you something — when you are chosen by God, He won't let you quit! You are in partnership with God and when one person in the relationship sees the other getting weak; they'll encourage and push them to keep going. God will always encourage us to keep going.

God used Gabriel greatly in my life to sow seeds of encouragement. I remember, when he left his job on short notice, I did not have a chance to say farewell. At that moment, I knew that his assignment was up, and he had deposited everything and completed what he had been called to do.

Also, during that time, God opened the doors for me to receive training in ministry at one of the most unlikely places — work. I joined a Bible study that was held at my workplace. I attended for over a year and became very close to the leaders of the group; a married couple, who were both local pastors in the area. God spoke to one of the pastors of the Bible Study and gave her specific instructions. She told us that God had laid certain people on her heart that she needed to ask to teach the Bible studies, and I was one of the people. I remember she said, "This is preparing you guys for your ministries." She believed that God had great things in store for us.

I thank God for her and for allowing me to have that opportunity because it was in this group that I learned that God spoke to me prophetically. I would be preparing for the Bible study and in the middle of preparing my outlines for the lesson, "*boom!*" — a Word of the Lord would come to mind and I would write it down immediately. It felt so natural and there was nothing spooky or deep about it. This would happen quite frequently. It flowed and as I continued to write, I noticed that it felt as if whatever was bothering me was healed. When God begins to develop you in your gifting, I believe it will feel natural. There will be no striving to bring it about; it will flow from what God has already placed on the inside of you.

God brought these wonderful people across my path to encourage me and to mentor me. God knows exactly what you need for every season of your life. Sometimes, He will bring people across your path and other times you may be in a season where you may not have any mentors. If this is you, remember that we have the ultimate mentor and that is the Holy Spirit. John 14:26 says,

**"The Advocate, the Holy Spirit,
whom the Father will send in my name,
will teach you all things and will
remind you of everything
I have said to you."**

You will be surprised at some of the mentors and people that God will bring along the way to speak into your life during your journey. It's exciting! Get ready for an exciting time with God, for the great encounters, and Kingdom Alliances.

Treasures of Truth

Realize that God is sovereign and all-knowing. He is strategic and knows that you will need help and encouragement to complete the great task and call that He has ahead for you.

In Colossians 4:10-14, a man by the name of Epaphras counseled many people in the Colossian church. Even after his assignment was up and he moved to another city, he still warred in prayer for the Colossian church. God will send people into your life or may even send you to mentor, encourage and support. Know that you are not alone because God has people here to help you fulfill your assignment.

Today I Will...

- Ask God to bring great encounters and Kingdom alliances into my life — when He knows I need it.
- Trust in the ultimate mentor, the Holy Spirit — the Counsellor who will encourage, lead and mentor me in all aspects of my life.

Let's Pray...

Loving God, I thank You for Divine connections and Kingdom alliances. I pray for the right alignments in my life and in Your ordained times and seasons. I ask you Lord, let me always be in the right place at the right time. Thank you for placing the right people in my path.

In Jesus' Name,

Amen.

DEVOTION 4

God's Timing – God's Process

"Each young woman's turn came to go in to King Ahasuerus after she had completed twelve months' preparation, according to the regulations for the women, for thus were the days of their preparation apportioned: Six months with oil of myrrh, and six months with perfumes and preparations for beautifying women. *Thus prepared*, each young woman went to the king, and she was given whatever she desired to take with her from the women's quarters to the king's palace."
(Esther 2:12-13, NKJV)

Do you sometimes feel like skipping the process? Do you feel alone in the wait? God is still there; He wouldn't just leave you. Like you, I have been tempted several times to want to skip the process and bypass the delays. Even in a very practical sense, most times when I'm getting ready to read a new book, I will naturally skim the table of contents and read the book summary to get an idea of what the book is about. I will then start reading the first chapter and notice that I'll become impatient with the *process* of reading the entire book and having to wait to find out the outcome. I find myself turning to the last few chapters to see how things end — but God doesn't allow us to do this in life.

If God showed us everything He has planned for our lives, it would blow our socks off! He wants to make sure we are fully processed and ready to handle where He is taking us and what He plans to do in our lives. Do you know how important the beginning and middle chapters are? Very important. It is in those moments that you learn things about God and yourself. This is where you are being made into that good soldier that endures hardship. You find out what you're made of and learn things about yourself that you would have never known if you had decided to just skip to the end.

I remember walking into my place of employment one day, carrying quite a few things. I had my laptop bag, a bag full of healthy snacks for the workweek, and my purse. These items were heavy on my arms, and there were several people walking into the building with me. While walking, I noticed that some of the people were quite a few steps ahead of me and I thought, "Wow, why am I so far behind them?"

At that moment, the Holy Spirit began to speak to me. He said, *"Renee, look at the person in front of you. Look at what he is carrying."* He only had a small bag in his hand. Then the Holy Spirit said, *"Look at the lady all the way in the front. Look at what she's carrying,"* and I noticed that it was a lighter load. He began to minister to me and the thought came, *"What you're carrying is so great, it needs time to process. You may feel like you are further behind others, but you are right on track — not a minute early or late."*

I find that God is big on *process* with me in my journey because He wants me to be ready for where He is taking me, and the same for you — He wants *you* to be ready. It has been said by many: Don't be so quick to run to the spotlight because you are running to pressure, adversity, warfare, and all types of responsibility that you need to be processed and ready for — what a sobering thought!

Treasures of Truth

Sometimes, you may feel like your journey is taking longer than others, but then you have to ask yourself, "What am I carrying? What did God place on the inside of me?" In 2 Corinthians 4:7, it says that we have these hidden treasures in earthen vessels, and God has put every gift on the inside of you. Only God can process and birth those treasures out of you in His perfect timing.

Don't be impatient to skip to the end chapters. Trust God and trust in His process — He will place you in your destiny in His timing.

**"But we have this treasure in jars of clay
to show that this all-surpassing power
is from God and not from us."
(2 Corinthians 4:7, NIV)**

Today I Will...

- Remember that the gifts and treasures inside of me come from God. He will process them and birth them in His time.
- Meditate on the thought that God's timing is perfect. He is always on track — not a minute early nor a minute late.
- Ask God to grant me patience and perseverance during the process, to let His timing become my timing.

Let's Pray...

Heavenly Father, I ask that You would cause me to walk in a manner that is worthy of the calling to which I have been called with all humility, gentleness, and patience. Help me to realize that the end of a thing is better than its beginning and is worth the wait.

In Jesus' Name,

Amen.

DEVOTION 5

Just When You Think It's Over!

**"'For I know the plans I have
for you," says the Lord.
'They are plans for good and not for disaster,
to give you a future and a hope.'"
(Jeremiah 29:11, NLT)**

Another good lesson that God taught me about the importance of my journey was back in 2002, when I was preparing to attend college right after high school. Now, during this season of my life, I became afraid of the future. All I knew was high school and the thought of college scared me. I remember waiting late in the game to apply to different colleges, not because I was being lazy, but I was just scared about the next step. Finally, I remember deciding that I wanted to attend Oral Roberts University, and my mother and I began preparing the paperwork for my application.

Later that month, I received a letter in the mail stating that I had not been accepted and that they had an overwhelming amount of applications. I was encouraged to apply the next year. I felt crushed and I went to my room and cried. My mother came up and encouraged me and said that I should transfer the next year and that God was still in control.

During the last few weeks of school, almost everyone in my senior class was planning to go away to their respective universities and move into the dorms — and I felt stuck in my home state. One of my classmates began to brag about her acceptance in a school far away and said that you needed to stay in the dorms and on campus to get the "full college experience." She knew that I had not been accepted into the school of my choice and that I would have to stay home to attend community college. Before I go any further, I would like to encourage those of you who may be attending a community college right now. There is nothing wrong with staying local, especially if God is leading you to do so. However, during that season in my life, I was hurt and became angry because I felt that other people were moving forward and I was being delayed.

Although there was an impediment, I believe that experience taught me the importance of perseverance and fighting for what you want. By the grace of God, I did not give up on my plans to attend ORU.

After finishing my first year of community college, I remember calling the registrar's office at ORU and notifying them of my completion of the classes for my freshman year. I found out that I was six credits short of transferring for the upcoming fall. I felt powerless and shed some tears and ended up going to sleep. When I woke up, I heard the Holy Spirit say so loudly in my spirit, *"Wilmington College."* Now I didn't know anything about this college, let alone the name, until the Holy Spirit brought it to my attention, and I found the number in the yellow pages and decided to call. I explained my situation and found two classes that would satisfy my requirement to transfer over to ORU, and this process would be very smooth.

After getting registered and accepted into Wilmington College's summer semester, I am happy to tell you that I received a "Conditional Acceptance" from ORU for the fall semester. After completing the six credits from Wilmington

University, I received a full acceptance into ORU. Initially, it was a very intense battle to get into ORU and the devil brought many roadblocks along the way to discourage me. However, God opened that door for me. I remember walking into ORU with not a lot and coming out with more than what I had when I started — that was so God! He gave me favor and caused me to not only graduate with my bachelor's degree in Business Management, but also a Master of Business Administration in Business Administration in 2009, and I am so thankful.

I needed to learn perseverance because of the journey ahead. Looking back, I can now say that getting rejected from ORU back in 2002 was one of the best things that could have happened to me. That experience taught me how to be strong in God and keep going no matter what obstacles stood in my way. Never allow the devil to make you feel like you don't deserve what you want! Keep trusting in God's plans, keep fighting, and keep running the race that He has laid out for you!

Treasures of Truth

In Ecclesiastes 7:8, we read: "The end of a matter is better than its beginning, and patience is better than pride." Remember, it's not how you start, but how you finish. Trust in God's plans for you. He knows the beginning and He knows the end — He has it all under control. Remember that God is a rewarder of those who diligently seek Him, so keep seeking Him in all that you do.

Today I Will...

- Remind myself that my Heavenly Father has plans to prosper and not to harm me. Plans to give me a future and a hope.
- Trust in His wisdom as the Master Planner and the Author and Finisher of my faith.
- Believe that although I may not have started well, my Heavenly Father will allow me to finish well.

Let's Pray...

Almighty God, I thank You because You have already fashioned and planned out my days. Father God, give me perseverance and resolve to know that You have already been in my future. Help me to always remember that my footsteps are ordered by You, and my future is in Your hands. I thank You because You are watching over Your Word in my life, and it will not return back to You void.

In Jesus' Name,

Amen.

God is Sovereign

**"Blessed are you when people hate you
and when they exclude you and revile
you and spurn your name as evil,
on account for the Son of Man!
Rejoice in that day, and leap for joy,
for behold, your reward is great in heaven;
for so their fathers did to the prophets."
(Luke 6:22-23)**

I am sure that many of you reading this book have experienced rejection — some deeper than others — but I can definitely relate. As a kid, I endured extreme bullying at the tender age of thirteen. Satan used this to try to silence my voice and bring poor self-esteem and insecurity into my life.

I came from a sheltered home and grew up in a wonderful church in my home state. However, during the early teen years of my life, I did not have any friends and I remember the warfare being so intense for me. The devil always used girls to target and bully me, and the sad part is that some of those people were very close to me. Many girls didn't like me because they thought I was trying to talk to their boyfriends, and some had no reason at all for disliking me. I was gossiped about and I remember hiding in the bathroom so that I wouldn't get jumped. Other times, I was spat on and punched in front of almost the entire school.

The devil used these experiences to try to break me, and I didn't understand why I was going through this and no one else seemed to be experiencing bullying. I just wanted to stay under the radar, but Satan influenced certain people to target me every day. I became a people-pleaser and learned how to say just the right thing to keep people at peace with me. I felt like I was always walking on eggshells. That was not God; He has called us to be free!

I never told my parents how badly I was being bullied because I knew they had bills and many concerns of their own, and I didn't want to add any stress to them. I learned how to cope with the bullying by internalizing things and not really expressing how I felt.

There was really only one person that I was able to share my experiences with and she has gone on to be with the Lord. Essie L. Bronson was my great aunt and a strong woman of God with a compassion-filled heart. She lived with my family and would take care of my siblings and me when we were very little. She was the type of person who really cared about you and what was going on in your life. If there was something that bothered you, she would sit and pray for you, and hug and cry with you. I remember talking to her and telling her about my bullying experience, crying about it and pouring my heart out to her — and she did not judge me. I felt the love of God through this amazing woman. She sat there and listened to everything that I was saying; and when I cried, she cried too and prayed with me. I just love her, and I will never forget how she helped me through that tough time in my life. I think it's important to express yourself and find someone that you can trust to share your heart with, but do allow the Holy Spirit to guide you to the right person.

I believe God allowed the bullying to happen because when I was thirteen, God knew what I would encounter at thirty. He was just allowing it to prepare me for leadership, for not being liked, and to learn how to keep on ticking when no one was walking by my side except for Him — He taught me how to be strong! Nothing is ever wasted with God. If you are being bullied; there is a purpose. You never know where God is going to take you!

Treasures of Truth

If you are going through a difficult season, whether it be bullying or persecution in another form, remember that God is the God of detail. Nothing escapes His notice and He has a plan and a purpose even in the hardest of times. The fact that He is allowing you to go through this season means that He has a reason for your season. Some of the things that you may be experiencing now, God may use ten or even twenty years down the line so that you are ready for the great call that He has on your life. Therefore, endure hardness as a good soldier. Remember that you are chosen by God, and what Satan thinks he can use to break you, God is going to use to bring deliverance to many and dismantle the power of darkness through your life.

Today I Will...

- Remember that all things happen for a purpose and that nothing is ever wasted in my life.
- Know that God is the God of detail and the fact that He has allowed me to be in this season or experience will ultimately be for my benefit in the future.
- Know that I am chosen by God and what the enemy has planned to break me, God is going to use mightily for His glory.

Let's Pray...

All-Knowing Father, help me recognize that You have the right people who are supposed to be connected to my life. Please help me to realize that the other people's choices aren't a reflection of me. Also, help me to guard my heart and not become bitter from the rejection of others, but to know that I am accepted and a part of the Beloved.

In Jesus' Name,

Amen.

DEVOTION 7

The Escape Plan

"In you, LORD, I have taken refuge;
let me never be put to shame;
deliver me in your righteousness.
Turn your ear to me, come
quickly to my rescue;
be my rock of refuge, a strong
fortress to save me.
Since you are my rock and my fortress,
for the sake of your name lead and guide me.
Keep me free from the trap that is set for me,
for you are my refuge."
(Psalms 31:1-4, NIV)

Remember the time when I experienced bullying? Now, the devil was very shrewd during this particular time in my life, and the bullying shifted from certain girls to the most popular guy in school. This guy liked me but I did not like him in a romantic way. I was only thirteen and I had crushes on celebrities and boybands at that time. Since I didn't give this young man the attention he wanted, he began to pick on me and make rude remarks to me in front of everyone. Some of the things he said were so mean, and I had reached my breaking point.

I went home that day and asked myself, "What can I do to get this guy to stop picking on me?" And the thought ran through my mind: "Just have sex with him and he will leave you alone. Give him what he wants." And I thought, "Yes, I'll do it so I can get some relief at school."

Now, you and I both know that this thought came from the enemy and it was wrong! But at that time, I didn't realize it. I was eager to get some peace. I agreed to meet this guy behind the school, and I was so afraid of what was about to occur — I was just a little girl. I did not see my worth and value, and I was just going to give away my virginity to some guy, so I could stop being bullied. I had decided that I wasn't going to share this decision with anyone. Satan tried to get me to negotiate with him, but it was at the expense of something that was so precious, and precious in the sight of God — my purity. I remember the sunbeams shining on me and I could feel the warmth of the rays on my arms. I felt like God was letting me know that He saw me and that I couldn't hide from Him what I was planning to do. The sun started to shine directly on the spot where we were standing. At that moment, a boy on his bike came riding toward us. He said, "You both need to get inside. The teacher is looking for you." This young man was a classmate who knew the guy that I had agreed to meet but I didn't know the boy at all, he was just from my school.

Let me tell you, God sent that young man to come around the school to get me out of that situation! If he hadn't come, I could have fallen pregnant at thirteen years old. The devil wanted to bring turmoil and pain into my life and he wanted to steal my future, but God said, "Not so." God saw my worth even when I didn't see it, and He protected it and me, even when I was willing to give it away.

**"O Lord, you have examined my heart
and know everything about me.
You know when I sit down or stand up.
You know my thoughts even
when I'm far away.
You see me when I travel
and when I rest at home.**

> You know everything I do.
> You know what I am going to say
> even before I say it, Lord.
> You go before me and follow me.
> You place your hand of blessing on my head.
> Such knowledge is too wonderful for me,
> too great for me to understand!"
> (Psalm 139: 1-6, NLT)

Treasures of Truth

Ladies and gentlemen, please protect your purity — it has great value. Some of you may be saying, "Well, I already gave away my purity." The good thing about God is that He forgives, and when He forgives you, He cleanses and washes you of every mistake or shortcoming and puts it in the sea of forgetfulness! He acts as if it never happened. He moves on past the mistake and so should you. There is no condemnation to those who are in Christ Jesus!

Today I Will...

- Not negotiate with the devil concerning things in my life, but always go to God for prayer and guidance and know that He has a victorious comeback for me.
- Realize that I am chosen and protected. There are certain parameters in my life that the enemy can't cross.
- Trust in God's Character and know that He will not leave me. Since I belong to Him, He will always provide a way of escape.

Let's Pray...

Heavenly Father, I thank You for Your unfailing love and grace. Help me to see that You are several steps ahead of the enemy. I thank You because nothing ever escapes Your notice, and You see my afflictions and will deliver me out of them all. You have not given me into the hands of the enemy but have set my feet into a spacious place.

In Jesus' Name,

Amen.

DEVOTION 8

God's Power is Stronger Than Your Kryptonite

**"For who *is* God, except the Lord?
And who *is* a rock, except our God?
It is God who arms me with strength,
And makes my way perfect."
(Psalm 18:31-32, NKJV)**

Remember the Bible study at work? Well, one particular day, we were discussing areas of weakness. A colleague said that he asked God to take away one of his struggles, and God said, *"No, I'm not going to take it away because My grace is sufficient for you."* At that moment, I realized that God is stronger than your kryptonite or areas of weakness.

For many years, because of the bullying and rejection in my past, I struggled with insecurity and the fear of man. I asked God to help me overcome this area in my life and thought that He would just take it away — but God had another plan in mind. He says in His Word:

**"But he said to me, 'My grace is
sufficient for you,
for my power is made perfect in weakness.'
Therefore I will boast all the more
gladly about my weaknesses, so that
Christ's power may rest on me."
(2 Corinthians 12:9)**

Over several years of my career, I noticed that God would cause me to receive favor with those in leadership. He began to challenge that area of insecurity in me, and I was pushed out in the forefront of my coworkers at an accelerated rate.

I was offered various jobs in leadership positions where I had to manage a group of people, and in those roles, I had to depend on God every step of the way. You see, I learned early on that God will make you face head-on, the very thing that you are afraid of or the area in your life that requires His grace.

I remember always telling myself, "Renee, you couldn't make it working in a that large city. It's such a fast-paced environment with extremely competitive people, and you wouldn't fit in." This was the insecurity talking and I didn't think that

God noticed but He did, and He opened a great door of opportunity for me to accept a job in a large metropolitan area. Can you guess what kind of job it was? It was a job in a leadership role! I remember, before accepting this job, I was afraid and second-guessed myself and wondered if it was even God.

This took me back to the time when I was in college. In order to graduate, we had to take a swimming proficiency test. Of course, I was one of those people who didn't know how to swim. I remember when it was my turn: I walked up to the ledge and my knees were shaking. I looked at how deep the water was and began to walk away. Then, I heard my teacher's voice. She spoke with confidence and said, "Renee, I'm right here. I promise, I won't let anything happen to you. If I see you go to the bottom, I will swim down and get you. You'll be fine. I promise, I'm here." Then she went on to say, "If you jump in head first, you will come right up to the top. Your body already knows what to do. It's just all in your head. Shut down the fear. Don't think; just do it." After hearing those words, I jumped in not once but twice and passed my swimming test!

Just like the teacher in the swimming class, God definitely reassured me that He would be with me when I walked through this new door of opportunity. God confirmed that this opportunity was from Him, and it was confirmed by several people that didn't even know about it. Then inside, I heard the Lord say, *"You need to walk through this door. Walk through the door even if you feel nervous. I will be with you,"* and I did.

There were many people that told me that they didn't think I was ready for the new opportunity, but the Lord told me to walk right through the door anyway. You see, you have to be careful when listening to many voices because if I had listened to the wrong voice, I could have missed His blessing. Listen to God's voice. He will be there right with you. Now, I don't say this to brag, but only to encourage. I had only been working in this career field for about eight years and went up the career ladder very fast. The Lord blessed me with this promotion that took others over twenty years to reach. That was definitely the favor of God, and I am so thankful for it. He is not a respecter of persons; if He did it for me, He can definitely do it for you.

God has definitely refined me in the area of insecurity and the fear of man, and it has only been by His grace because His grace is more than enough. Do you know what grace means? It is the free and unmerited favor of God. By His grace, God will give you the ability and strength to do things that are impossible for you to do on your own so that you know it's Him. On my journey, I have learned that it is important to God to show me that through Him I can overcome anything. I have become stronger in my mindset and the way that I see myself. I look through a new lens now, and that is the Word of God. God wants you to claim the victory in every area of your life today. I received my breakthrough, and you will too.

Treasures of Truth

Sometimes, when we have areas of weakness, it can become such a struggle that the weakness is all that we can see. It becomes like kryptonite to Superman: we feel helpless. However, God is Omnipotent which means "All Powerful." He is way more powerful than any kryptonite in your life and He can empower you to overcome all of your weaknesses. Know that when you have areas of weakness, it's an opportunity for God to show His strength through you — when you do overcome that area of weakness, you will know that it's only through His power that you are victorious and that's how He is glorified in your life!

Today I Will...

- Not elevate my weakness over God's ability and power, and trust that God can and will deliver
- Expect to be empowered by the power of the Holy Spirit to overcome these weaknesses in my life.
- Recognize that the areas of weakness in my life are just areas of opportunity for God to show His strength through me and be glorified in my life!

Let's Pray...

Heavenly Father, I ask that You will endow me with Your power. I ask that Your overflowing grace and anointing will be so strong in my life, that it will cause the forces and powers of the enemy to be destroyed and dismantled. I receive Your grace today.

In Jesus' Name,

Amen.

DEVOTION 9

Separated, But Not Alone

**"But know that the Lord hath set
apart him that is godly for himself:
the Lord will hear when I call unto him."
(Psalm 4:3, KJV)**

Every great leader experiences seasons of silence and loneliness from the world. God will sometimes take you from among the masses, just so that He can speak to you and tell you who you really are.

Let's go back to Genesis when Adam walked in the garden, in the cool of the day with God. What do you think God was saying to Adam during that time? He was probably telling him who he was and his purpose. I heard a very well-known pastor say that when you see any great leader, thank God for them passing the test. Great leaders experience persecution, rejection, and periods of loneliness. Look at some of the great men and women in the Bible. Moses was in the desert for some time, Joseph was sold as a slave, the Apostle Paul was thrown in jail, and Daniel's prayer was held up, but he waited for an answer.

In your journey, you will find that you may go through seasons of being set apart — I know, as I definitely have. Let me tell you why you are going through this: it is because you are being refined and molded for a great work for the Lord. I remember when I first attended Oral Roberts University; one of the senior leaders spoke in a chapel service and said, "God will take you out of an environment away from everyone and all of the voices, just so you can hear from Him." I had never been to Tulsa, Oklahoma and knew nothing about the area, but that is where God began to speak to me the most. Never despise those seasons of seclusion from man because this is where God reveals His mysteries to you.

"For many are called, but few are chosen."
(Matthew 22:14, NLT)

Treasures of Truth

Embrace this time of intimacy with God and allow Him to reveal Himself and His secrets to you. Know that it's in these seasons that God will reveal deep things to you. Always remember, you are never alone — Jesus said that He will never leave you nor forsake you!

Today I Will...

- Embrace this season of being set apart — it is an opportunity to draw my strength, my wisdom and every need from God. My dependency and my sufficiency comes from Him. Sometimes, when God elevates me, there is no one else with me; just God and me.
- Realize that sometimes, elevation does require separation.
- Meditate on the fact that I am never alone because He has promised to never leave me nor forsake me.

Let's Pray...

Heavenly Father, thank you for choosing me. Help me to realize that nothing in my life happens haphazardly, but You've intently designed the blueprint for my life. You have designated the set seasons for my development and growth in You. Help me to embrace and get all that I need to get out of this season of being set apart for You.

In the Matchless Name of Jesus,

Amen.

DEVOTION 10

Developing the Champion Within

**"Finally, be strong in the Lord
and in the strength of his might."
(Ephesians 6:10)**

In a perfect world, you would get everything you need and in the most comfortable environment where everyone liked you and wanted to see you succeed. This is not the case for most people, especially not for me.

Sometimes, God will allow you to be in environments where people are not always nice and can come across as mean and harsh, and don't always deliver the information you need in the kindest way. I don't believe that God is trying to make your life difficult or intentionally bring things your way to sabotage you because that is not His character. The Bible says in Proverbs 13:15 (KJV), "Good understanding giveth favor: but the way of the transgressor is hard." We are not transgressors, but His righteous people, and with His grace, He will cause us to win in life. However, I do believe that God does allow seasons and experiences that did not always seem good at the time to work together for your good. These experiences make you stronger, and God doesn't want us to ever have a mentality of giving up, no matter what obstacle is standing in our way.

I never understood why it always felt as if I was being attacked or disliked by most of my coworkers and never got the assistance from them that I needed. I even received push-back from my manager and I know he wanted me to fail. God sometimes allows these things to occur, so that our faith in Him can become stronger than ever. These opportunities also enable God to cause us to come out on top — no matter who doesn't want to help or see us succeed.

All that matters is that God wants to see you succeed. The Scripture says in 1 John 4:4, "You, dear children, are from God and have overcome them because the one who is in you is greater than the one who is in the world." You and God are the majority, period. You will always come out on top with God and He wants to show you that He'll have your back, even when no one else will. These experiences cause you to develop a thick skin and develop the champion within.

We are not weak people! We are strong in the power of His might. God wants us to come up higher in our thinking. He is strong in His mind, and He wants the same for us. God is not depressed, God does not grow weary, God is not timid, God is not insecure! As a matter of fact, the Bible says,

**"The wicked plot against the righteous
and gnash their teeth at them;
but the Lord laughs at the wicked,
for he knows their day is coming."
(Psalm 37: 12-13)**

God laughs in the face of His enemies because He knows the end from the beginning. He is confident!

Let's come up higher in our thinking and mirror our Father in Heaven. Remember who you are! You are strong — it is the way God designed you. My encouragement is to go through this season like a champ. You could be very well going through this process because of the relationships, platforms, and opportunities that God has lined up in the future for you.

Treasures of Truth

Remember that God hems you in, in front and behind (Psalm 139:5). He has got your back and is with you through every situation. You are being groomed and fashioned for your assignment and a great call from the Lord.

Rest in the fact that God will not put more on you than you can bear — you are stronger than you think because the GREATER ONE lives on the inside of you.

Today I Will...

- Remember that I win! The Lord is grooming and fashioning me for my assignment and a great call from Him.
- Change my mentality and know that He that is in me is greater than he that is in the world. I can do all things through Christ who strengthens me.
- Be transformed by the renewing of my mind and mirror my Father in Heaven.

Let's Pray...

Heavenly Father, thank You for grooming me and making me a vessel of honor fit for Your use. Grant me Your grace as You refine my character and integrity through this season.

Build a firm foundation within me, so that I can handle the responsibilities that You have ahead of me. Thank You for developing and making me ready.

In Jesus' Name,
Amen.

The Spirit of Competitive Jealousy

"For we are not fighting against flesh-and-blood enemies, but against evil rulers and authorities of the unseen world, against mighty powers in this dark world, and against evil spirits in the heavenly places."
(Ephesians 6:12)

Growing up, I would constantly encounter people in school who were very competitive, jealous, and wanting to compete with me. This was like a thorn in my side. Remember how the Apostle Paul spoke about a thorn in his flesh? This was my thorn in the flesh. I remember feeling as if I didn't deserve what I had because I was around other people that didn't grow up in the same type of environment — and they were envious.

Satan would use young ladies in school to agitate me in the area of jealousy and competition. I noticed that it was always with women and, naturally, I just got along more with guys. I always remember receiving harsh treatment from women; not all, but most women who I encountered. I would encounter these people often when operating in leadership roles. A word of advice: If you are on a team and in leadership roles, and encounter people who operate in a competitive and jealous spirit, I would say to definitely pray in the Spirit, and ask the Lord to allow you to keep a pure heart. The Bible says, "Above all things, guard your heart for out of it flows the issues of life."

When you operate from a pure heart, the anointing and power can flow freely, and lives will be changed. However, our enemy, Satan, does not want lives to change and he knows that you carry the goods. There is something so great on the inside of you and he wants to allow bitterness, anger, and fear to try to creep in so you won't be effective.

Now, back to my story, one particular day, I remember feeling so angry! That day, I had conducted a presentation for work and one of the ladies in attendance tried to take over and clarify and present for me and I became angry. I took this matter to the Lord. A couple of weeks later, the young lady came back and apologized to me.

People may try to make you look bad, argue or debate with you, but don't argue with those people; pray for them. There will be times when the Lord will want you to speak up for yourself and other times He may want you to remain silent and let Him fight your battles. You are dealing with a spirit behind that person's behavior, and we have the authority to tell those evil spirits to go because the Holy One of Israel resides on the inside of you. The devil is petty and he will use anyone that walks in the flesh and they may be totally unaware of being used.

Another time, I went to my local grocery store to make some purchases and there was a young lady checking out everyone. She was just as pleasant and as courteous to the people in line but when I approached her, her whole demeanor and tone changed. It was strange because I didn't know this woman and she didn't know me, but I noticed that it was spiritual and it was that same evil spirit that I had seen years ago that began to manifest in this young lady. I was still kind, but as I walked away to my car, I began to speak with authority to the devil, and let him know that he was trespassing on God's property. I began to plead the Blood of Jesus over myself and then I felt peace. My flesh began to calm down.

The devil must have been mad about that because later that summer, I remember having a dream and that same evil spirit began to manifest in a young lady in my dream. She spoke very rudely towards me and then spoke in a very disrespectful tone towards my father, and that did it for me. I just remember getting up from my seat and grabbing this girl by the arm with such force and strength and getting her out of the room and closing the door in her face. Now, the girl looked terrified, because she thought I was going to hurt her badly. I was surprised at the strength that I had and I could tangibly feel it. Not only was the spirit afraid, but I was taken aback by the amount of strength that I had. I felt like, if I needed to, I could destroy this spirit because of the amount of power that I had. This was power from the Almighty, power from on high. God revealed to me that I took authority over that evil spirit and drove it out of where I was. There will be people that don't like you, yes, you, but a word of caution: *Look past the person and recognize that it is a spirit from the enemy.*

**"Behold, I have given you authority
to tread on serpents
and scorpions, and over all
the power of the enemy,
and nothing shall hurt you."
(Luke 10:19)**

Treasures of Truth

Remember to look past the person and realize that there is a spirit operating behind that person's behavior. The war is not with the person, but with the enemy. Keep your heart pure, do not allow yourself to become angry and bitter — choose to forgive. In 2 Corinthians 2:10-11, we read:

"Anyone you forgive, I also forgive. And what I have forgiven—if there was anything to forgive—I have forgiven in the sight of Christ for your sake, in order that Satan might not outwit us. **For we are not unaware of his schemes.**"

Beware of the devil's plans to get you to walk in unforgiveness towards others.

Today I Will...

- Be mindful that I have authority from God and I will intentionally use it.
- Look past the person and realize that there is a spirit operating behind what they are doing.
- Keep my heart pure and will choose to forgive. By the grace of God, I will not allow unforgiveness, bitterness, anger, and fear to fester in my heart.
- War and battle in the Spirit and not in my carnal flesh.

Let's Pray...

Heavenly Father, I plead the Blood of Jesus over myself right now. I thank You that You have me in Your hands and no one can pluck me out. I ask that You remove every evil spirit and principality of jealousy. I thank You that these spirits have no connection to me, my family, friends, job, resources, or anything connected to me. Send Your warring angels to contend on my behalf against these evil spirits. Heal and restore my heart from any hurts that have been caused by jealousy. I pray for my enemies now and ask that You would bless and save them now.

In Jesus' Name,

Amen.

DEVOTION 12

Surprised by God's Favor

**"Now God had caused the official to show
favor and compassion to Daniel."
(Daniel 1:9)**

When you encounter mean people who actively
work against you, remind yourself that God has
you there for a reason. At one time in my career,
I had a mean boss. He was actually going through
a divorce during that time of his life and for some
reason, he always gave me a hard time. He tried
to set me back by lowering my rating and telling
his supervisor that he didn't think I was ready to
receive an increased level in my certification in my
field of work. This is a big deal if you work in the
business field. An increased certification provides
more opportunities and allows individuals to grow
and climb the career ladder at an expedited pace.
The increased certification offered more skillsets
under one's belt, and allowed more complex
work assignments, as well as serving in more
leadership roles. My supervisor was having these

conversations with his supervisor behind my back, trying to undermine my progress and I was not aware that this was happening — but God knew.

God gave me so much favor with his supervisor! During one of the conversations, she said to him, "I thank you for your opinion, but I will be granting her an increased level of certification anyway. I have seen her work and she has a great work ethic." After this happened, I found out the details from a fellow coworker who knew everything that was going on. The supervisor allowed her to share all the details with me and I was blown away by the goodness of God. The head supervisor asked my direct supervisor (the one who was trying to undermine me) to provide me with my certification. Normally, the supervisors will gather the team together to honor the individual, but this wasn't the case with me. I came back to my workstation to find the certificate in an envelope lying on my desk. Later, my direct supervisor called me on the phone to let me know that it was there.

This reminds me of the story about Haman and Mordecai. The king made Haman honor Mordecai in front of everyone. See, when God is on your side, even your enemies have to yield to His plan. He definitely holds the king's heart in His hands and turns it wherever He pleases.

**"The king's heart is in the hand of the Lord,
as the rivers of water: he turneth
it whithersoever he will."
(Proverbs 21:1, KJV)**

The head supervisor was extremely tough on me and everyone in my department, but I thank God for her because she was preparing me for what was ahead. She told me that she wanted people to take me seriously, and to carry myself with professionalism and respect. I was shocked that God used this lady to bless me and show me favor because I didn't think she liked me. God will surprise you as to who He causes to show favor to you.

**"Let love and faithfulness never leave you;
bind them around your neck,
write them on the tablet of your heart.
Then you will win favor and a good name
in the sight of God and man."
(Proverbs 3: 3-4)**

Treasures of Truth

God is the God of the details. He is always working behind the scenes and perfecting everything concerning you, even things that you don't know about.

He is Omnipresent and Omnipotent — He knows when people are plotting against you, and He will straighten everything out!

Today I Will...

- Know within my spirit that God is always working behind the scenes and perfecting everything concerning me.
- Remember that He is the God of the details; He is the Master Planner and everything is under His control.
- Trust in His ability to work all things out for my good and for His glory!

Let's Pray...

Heavenly Father, I thank You that You are my sun and my shield and that You bestow favor and honor in my life. I thank You that Your favor goes before me and that You make all of the crooked places straight.

Also, thank You Lord for causing people to want to help me. I declare your favor over my job, finances, relationships, and my future.

In Jesus' Name,

Amen.

DEVOTION 13

Focus on God

"Jesus answered, 'If I want him to remain alive until I return, what is that to you? You must follow me.'"
(John 21:22)

In the above Scripture, Jesus was talking to Peter alone and calling him to follow Him. Peter turned and saw John following them, and Peter asked, "Lord, what about him?" Peter was wondering about John's walk with the Lord and what Jesus was calling John to do. This is what Jesus said in reply to Peter's question: "If I want him to remain alive until I return, what is that to you? **You must follow me.**"

Nowadays, finding out what other people are up to is just a click away. You can get so busy looking at other people and comparing where you are to where someone else is, that you start to worry and lose focus on what God is doing in your life for that particular season. I must admit that this has happened to me a few times. I've looked on Facebook and seen many of my friends in different stages of their lives, and I've started to worry and feel anxious because I felt that I should be where they are, in a similar season or life stage.

We must remember that the steps of a good man are ORDERED by the Lord and He delights in our way. We cannot compare our beginning to someone's ending or our ending to someone's beginning. We are all at different stages in our lives that have been ordained by God. When we compare ourselves to others, we allow envy, jealousy, anxiety, fear, and insecurity to fester in our hearts. We also find ourselves becoming critical and judgmental of others. The Bible says:

"Above all else, guard your heart,
for everything you do flows from it."
(Proverbs 4:23)

We are to GUARD our hearts above all else, and if that means removing yourself from social media or fasting from it for a season so that you can hear from God and work on yourself — then so be it! God calls each one of us to follow Him through the paths and stages that He has planned. Don't let anything rob you of being the best possible version of yourself.

"Because the Sovereign LORD helps me,
I will not be disgraced.
Therefore, I have set my face like a stone,
determined to do his will.
And I know that I will not be put to shame."
(Isaiah 50:7, NLT)

Treasures of Truth

God has the perfect plan and the perfect timetable for your life. Be patient with His timing. Don't try to move ahead of Him or do things on your own. Trust in His perfect Will. Set your face like a flint and run the race set before you, looking unto Jesus, not at others who may also be running. Focus on what God is telling *you* to do — *you* follow Him.

Today I Will...

- Learn to be patient with my progress and the plan that God has for my life.
- Not try to move ahead of Him or try to do things on my own.
- Realize that I am not on anyone's timetable, but God's.
- Set my face like a flint and focus on the race set before me. I will do what God is telling *me* to do.

Let's Pray...

Loving Father, I thank You for the call that You have on my life. I ask that You give me a mind to study to show myself approved; a workman that doesn't need to be ashamed. Help me to overcome the temptation of looking at others and comparing my walk to theirs. Strengthen me to set my face like a flint with laser focus and determination to fulfill that calling that You have on my life.

In Jesus' Name,

Amen.

DEVOTION 14

Open your Heart to God

"The Lord is near to those who are discouraged; he saves those who have lost all hope."
(Psalm 34:18)

One morning, I felt down in my spirit because feelings from the past began to resurface about an ex-boyfriend. I believe that God wanted those feelings to resurface so that He could bring wholeness and healing to my heart. Sometimes, we don't want to say how we really feel, and we just bury it. We can't hide anything from God, and He actually searches the deep things of our hearts. God wanted this pain to come to the surface and address it, so that it would be healed. I remember being so angry with this guy for hurting me and playing games, but I was also to blame. I could have moved on instead of staying for so long. That morning, God spoke to me and said, *"Renee, what's wrong?"* and I responded back and said, "My heart;

it's broken," and He said, *"I know."* He went on to say, *"I want to heal it, can I?"* and I responded back and said, "Yes, Lord."

**"He heals the broken-hearted
and bandages their wounds."
(Psalm 147:3)**

I believe that God is very concerned about your heart, and He notices when there is a blockage between you and Him. I had a blockage and didn't even think it was serious, but I carried the hurt for a few years. Later that summer, I remember God speaking to me again so clearly and He said, *"Renee, you have to forgive him. You have to."* In that moment, I chose to forgive and asked the Lord to help me with my emotions and feelings of anger, and He did and still does — I am a work in progress.

After making that decision to forgive, I could literally feel someone's prayers. I knew someone was praying for me in that very moment and the Holy Spirit brought to my mind that it was Jesus. The Bible says that He makes intercession for us and He goes before the Father and prays for us. My pastor calls Him our Chief Intercessor in Heaven! How awesome it is to have the Chief Intercessor praying for you! Prayers from Jesus will definitely get answered.

"Who is he that condemneth?
It is Christ that died, yea rather,
that is risen again,
who is even at the right hand of God,
who also maketh intercession for us."
(Romans 8:28, KJV)

Treasures of Truth

I just want to encourage you that Jesus is praying for you right now. He knows what you are going through. He knows about the heartbreak and the deep things in your heart that you haven't told anyone about — He knows it all and He cares. He wants you to cry out to Him, because He is your Abba, your Father, and your friend. He wants to bring total and complete healing to your life.

**"Trust in him at all times, you people;
pour out your hearts to him,
for God is our refuge."
(Psalm 62:8)**

Today I Will ...

- Ask the Holy Spirit to help me open my heart to His healing touch.
- Pray for courage to bring those hidden things to Him and pour out my heart to Him.
- Know that as I pour out my heart, He hears me, He loves me — and He will heal me.

Let's Pray ...

Loving Father, I open my heart to You and I ask that You put the pieces back together and restore joy and hope in my life. I trust You with my hurts and deep wounds and ask that You would complete a work in my heart. I thank You for giving me beauty for ashes and I believe that You have better things ahead of me.

In Jesus' Name,
Amen.

DEVOTION 15

Finding Your Tribe

**"From one man He has made every
nationality to live over the whole earth and
has determined their appointed times
and the boundaries of where they live."**
(Acts 17:26)

You will literally go through seasons in your life where you feel as if you don't fit. Like a piece to a puzzle, there is a spot specifically designed for that particular piece to fit and the word for you, my friend, is *alignment*.

God will allow you to go through seasons of your life where you might not feel like you fit and you feel out of place. God causes this to happen because you're changing; you're evolving and it might feel uncomfortable or out of control. But sometimes, it's God rocking the boat and moving you into a place that He will show you. He is aligning you with His Will — His purpose and His plan for your life.

What helped me when I went through this season of feeling out of place was being open to knowing that by following God's leading, I was not going to be the same person that I was before; I started that journey. I was going to be stronger, more refined, and with the right community of believers. His plan is to transform us into the image of His Son and He will move us to that place where He wants us to be at the right time.

We must always be Spirit-led when it comes to the Lord aligning us and leading us to our tribe. Allow Him to make the right connections because the Bible warns us:

"The one who walks with the wise
will become wise,
but a companion of fools will suffer harm."
(Proverbs 13:20, HCSB)

God alone knows the perfect fit for you and will align you with the right people at the right time. He will put you in your tribe.

Treasures of Truth

Seek the guidance of the Holy Spirit with all your connections. Pray that He will align your path with the right people and that He will open the door of opportunity for you to connect with them. God has the right relationships lined up for you now and in the future.

Today I Will...

- Seek the guidance of the Holy Spirit to direct my path to the right connections today and in the days to come.
- Trust the Lord to put me in my tribe, in His perfect timing.
- Pray that I am in the right place, at the right time and that God will open up the doors of opportunity for right relationships.

Let's Pray...

Father, I thank you that You have the right relationships lined up for me now and in the days to come. I pray that You will open up those doors of opportunity to be at the right place, at the right time — to connect with the right people. Put me in my tribe — the tribe that You have prepared.

In Jesus' Name, I pray,

Amen.

DEVOTION 16

Be Slow to Speak

**"Set a guard, O Lord, over my mouth;
Keep watch over the door of my lips."
(Psalm 141:3, NKJV)**

Back in college, I remember sharing something very personal with a classmate who I esteemed as a very spiritual and mature young leader. After being vulnerable with this person, she encouraged and prayed with me, and even shared her perspective. However, I later noticed that she then began distancing herself from me, and some of her friends did the same. At the time, I took it personally and felt hurt by it, because I was reaching out for help and encouragement. Over time, the Lord told me that I needed to forgive her and to move past it. He also let me know that He did not direct me to share that personal information with this young lady. I learned a valuable lesson from that incident.

**"My dear brothers and
sisters, take note of this:
Everyone should be quick to listen,
slow to speak
and slow to become angry,
because human anger does not produce
the righteousness that God desires."
(James 1:19-20)**

The Bible says to be slow to speak and quick to listen for a reason. You really have to watch and listen to people. Don't be so quick to share your innermost thoughts and heart with them. Now, I am not saying that everyone is out to get you but you have to be aware of people because everyone is not mature enough to handle what you share with them, and we are all but flesh. God does not want His children to be used and taken advantage of, so take your time with people. Be very selective about who you allow into your inner circle. Consult the Holy Spirit, the Guide on the inside, with your every move and He'll lead you on the right path.

Treasures of Truth

Always go to God first and allow Him to lead you to the right person. Sometimes, some things are just best to be kept between you and the Lord — after all, He can handle every part of you.

"The wise don't tell everything they know, but the foolish talk too much and are ruined." (Proverbs 10:14)

Today I Will...

- Be slow to speak and quick to listen. Slow to speak to others and quick to listen to God's Spirit.
- Pray that God would place a guard over my mouth. To only share what He would want me to share, with whom He would want me to share it.
- Use discernment and allow the Lord to guide me on what to say, when to say it, and who to speak to.
- Cast all my cares and burdens on Him — He is more than able to handle every part of me.

Let's Pray...

Heavenly Father, I ask that You grant me spiritual wisdom. Cause me to be as wise as a serpent and as harmless as a dove. Allow me to use wisdom on what to share and when to share it.

Thank You for the Holy Spirit who will lead me and guide me into all truth.

In Jesus' Name,

Amen.

DEVOTION 17

Accepted, Approved, and Affirmed

**"To the praise of the glory of his grace,
wherein he hath made us
accepted in the beloved."
(Ephesians 1:6)**

I like to watch celebrity interviews and get a sense of their background and learn what has shaped them. One day, I was watching an interview with a well-known inspirational speaker and she shared her powerful story.

She was saying that when growing up, she always wanted to be chosen by a man and become someone's wife because she grew up with "daddy" issues. Now, I didn't grow up with "daddy" issues because I grew up in a home with both my parents where I received love and attention. However, I grew up as a rejected child — remember the bullying experience at school? Well, I experienced rejection from my society and the outside world. I never fitted in. Like the celebrity that I referred to earlier, I've always had that longing and desire to be chosen or accepted by someone.

It is natural to want everyone to like you but it can be unhealthy if we use this as a way to feel validated and accepted. I didn't realize that all along, I had already been chosen and accepted by God. Not realizing how much He already loved me and that I am ENOUGH because He made me. I come from Him. I am His and He is mine.

**"In him we were also chosen, having been predestined according to the plan of him who works out everything in conformity with the purpose of his will, in order that we, who were the first to put our hope in Christ, might be for the praise of his glory."
(Ephesians 1:11)**

Treasures of Truth

Only God can define who you really are at your core — your identity comes from Him. Be careful in allowing other people to define who you are. When you know that you belong to Him, you move from feeling rejected to knowing you are accepted. And if God be for you, who can be against you?

**"You, dear children, are from God
and have overcome them, because
the one who is in you is greater than
the one who is in the world."
(1 John 4:4)**

Today I Will...

- Be aware more than ever that I am loved, accepted, and already approved by Almighty God.
- Realize that my identity comes from Him alone.
- Know that greater is He that is in me, than he that is in the world. God is for me!

Let's Pray...

Heavenly Father, I receive Your love and acceptance. I thank You that You chose me before the very foundations of the world. Keep me as the apple of Your eye. Thank You that my identity comes from You. I forgive everyone that offended me and ask You to bless and save them now.

In Jesus' Name,

Amen.

DEVOTION 18

Direction in the Selection

**"If you need wisdom, ask our generous
God, and he will give it to you.
He will not rebuke you for asking."
(James 1:5, NLT)**

When God gives you someone special to be your spouse, He will give you a man or a woman with purpose — a Kingdom purpose. You'll definitely see the upgrade in your life, because the Bible says that the blessing of the Lord will make you rich and add no type of sorrow to your life. It sounds like God has some kings and queens in the earth that He will connect to fulfill His Divine purpose on Earth. We must be so careful to allow the Holy Spirit to guide us in this area of our life.

I would like to share my own personal testimony. I was very hardheaded in the area of dating in my early 20's and said, "God, you can have every area of my life — except for dating. I will take care of this area of my life." Let me tell you how foolish that was! I kept going in circles and meeting the same type of guy time after time. There is a Scripture in the Bible that says, "He gives grace to the humble but resists the proud," reference James 4:6. I always thought that Scripture was geared towards the arrogant and really mean people, but I realized that I was being prideful towards God by saying, "I'm smarter than You in this area and I don't need Your help." I was proud and it caused me to go through wrong relationships and experience heartbreaks time and time again.

After recognizing this cycle, I went to the Lord in prayer. The Holy Spirit brought conviction and caused me to humble myself before the Lord. I asked for His help and asked Him why this cycle kept going on over and over again, and He said, *"Renee, I never told you to date any of those guys. You didn't even include Me in your selection process."* That part of the Scripture that says He resists the proud means that He doesn't help people that are prideful because they push Him away. He will sometimes allow life and situations to humble you to let you know that He is always necessary — God is so necessary!

Even in my disobedience, I still saw the goodness of God. He protected me in those bad relationships and provided a way of escape every time. That was the goodness of God and speaks to His character. He could have become angry and said, "Forget her," but He didn't throw me away during those years of my life. He covered me and knew that one day I would get it.

I'm saying all of this to you so that you won't make the same mistake that I did. After He revealed to me that I had not allowed Him into that area of my life, I began to weep, and I repented and asked for His forgiveness and help.

**"Godly sorrow brings repentance
that leads to salvation
and leaves no regret, but worldly sorrow
brings death."
(2 Corinthians 7:10)**

At that moment, He spoke in a still, small, quiet voice and said, *"What do you want me to do for you?"* My heart was overjoyed and I began to lay my petitions before the Lord, and I said, "God, I need help with this and I need help with that. I don't know what to do here and I need clarity on that." I knew He was listening to my every word and when I was finished praying, I felt a release. I knew it was already done in the Spirit.

Always remain humble before the Lord. We are not smart enough to make all of the right decisions for our lives. You may make good decisions, but who's to say it's always the best decision? Only God knows. We don't know it all, but God does. I know when I've tried to select someone who I thought would be good for me, I could only see how we'd look together in the present, but God could see the present and the future. God can see ten, twenty, and thirty years down the line, and He knows if this relationship will be good for you. You see, our knowledge is finite and limited compared to an Omniscient and All-knowing God. We need His wisdom and direction in the selection.

**"Trust in the Lord with all your heart
and lean not on your own understanding;
in all your ways submit to him,
and he will make your paths straight."
(Proverbs 3:5-6)**

Treasures of Truth

Remember to include God in your selection process. He knows what the future is going to hold and knows more about that person than you do. Ask Him to grant you wisdom in all your decisions. Remember, you are not alone and you can trust Him to bring the right person to you at the right time.

**"Oh, how great are God's
riches and wisdom and knowledge!
How impossible it is for us to understand
his decisions and his ways!"
(Romans 11:33, NLT)**

Today I Will...

- Humble myself before God and repent for where I have excluded Him from any area of my life.
- Invite God in and to come and take control — even the areas that I struggle to give to Him.
- Trust Him to direct my paths, to grant me wisdom, and help me to know His perfect Will for my life.

Let's Pray...

Almighty God, I ask for Your wise counsel and direction. I choose to trust You with all my heart, and not lean on my own understanding. I need You, God, and I thank You, that in Your appointed time You'll connect me to the right man or woman of God.

In Jesus' Name,

Amen.

DEVOTION 19

Superficial vs. Substance

**"But the Lord said to Samuel, 'Do not
consider his appearance or his height,
for I have rejected him. The Lord does
not look at the things people look at.
People look at the outward appearance,
but the Lord looks at the heart.'"
(1 Samuel 16:7, NIV)**

Desiring God's best in our lives causes us to value
substance over what is superficial. I would rather
have a man chasing after Jesus with a beautiful
heart than a man in a flashy suit, who looks good
on the outside, but not on the inside. I have been
blessed to have grown up around several men
of substance in my family and church. These
great examples have taught me that a person of
substance will have integrity, will treat your heart
with care and most importantly, will aim to live a life
of pleasing the Lord. On the surface, a superficial
person may tell you all the things that you want to
hear but does not have an intention of leading the

relationship to Christ. Rely on the Holy Spirit and think soberly.

I've met so many guys with lots of money. They have the looks, the cars, the social status, and popularity but they don't have Jesus. Jesus makes the difference. It doesn't matter how much money they have sitting in the bank or how good they look — if they don't have Jesus then it's not wise for them to be in your life.

I remember watching the Rocky series with my dad. Rocky III is my favorite. Now, in the movie, Rocky was preparing to fight Mr. T, who was very strong and intimidating, and Rocky began to lose faith in himself. He became afraid and insecure in his ability to fight against Mr. T. Also, during this time, his longtime coach, Mickey, passed away so he was grieving during his preparation for the fight with Mr. T. Now, Rocky's zeal and passion began to dwindle and his longtime friend, Apollo, who had been training him for the fight, noticed this decline and became frustrated with Rocky. He couldn't get through to him, but his wife did. During a scene in the movie, Adrienne talks to Rocky on the beach and when she speaks, you can feel that her words are coming directly from her heart. She knows her husband and cares about him. She asks him what he's afraid of and lets him know that the people that really matter and care about him will be by his side regardless. She challenges him to face and overcome this fear, and to do it for himself and not for anyone else. After watching that movie, I realized, wow, Rocky has a woman of substance.

Ladies, he may be fine; and guys, she may be fine but allow the Guide on the inside to lead you to the right one, because He looks beyond the surface; He looks at the heart. You want someone who can talk to the queen or king inside of you — that surpasses all of the money, all of the status, or whatever is on the surface. You want someone who will weather the storms of life with you. Someone who is looking through their spiritual lenses and looking past what they can see in the flesh, someone who is discerning and sensitive to the Spirit of God. You want a spouse of substance — a spouse that belongs to the Lord.

I am praying for you right now, that God will assign the right man and woman to you, and that you are aligned with purpose.

Treasures of Truth

Let's not just look at the surface, but at substance. Limiting your selection to superficial things like how much money a person has or how attractive they look on the outside as the only determining factors will indeed discredit you. You want someone that will weather the storms with you. Someone of substance, value, and worth. Remember, you are not alone. God, the All-knowing One, has already planned your future. He is the only one who can see inside a person's heart. Trust Him to bring the right person into your life.

Today I Will...

- Trust the Lord that He has the right person set apart for me, for His purpose, and plan.
- Pour out my heart to the Lord and tell Him all I need, knowing that He is listening to everything.
- Pray for my future spouse. I will pray that the Lord will work His good and perfect Will in his or her life.
- To the married: Today I will pray for my husband/wife. That he or she will become a man or woman of integrity and substance. That the Lord will move powerfully in his or her life and that His plan and purpose for our marriage would come into being.

Let's Pray...

Heavenly Father, I pray for a man or woman of substance with a beautiful spirit. May he or she be a person of integrity with a sincere and genuine heart. Allow this person to be filled with godly character and unconditional love. Lord, prepare me also to be the same and a blessing to this person's life.

In Jesus' Name,

Amen.

DEVOTION 20

Patience is Key

**"But let patience have her perfect work,
that ye may be perfect and
entire, wanting nothing."
(James 1:4)**

During the holiday break, I was in the car with my brother and we were driving to Walmart to pick up a few items. Once we reached our destination, we noticed that the parking lot had several options and open spaces to choose from. However, my brother didn't take the first spot that he saw. He kept driving and took his time. Once we drove around, we noticed a parking space up front and center, so close to the entrance of the store. My brother then said, "See what happens when you take your time and you are patient? You can make the best choices."

That was so powerful to me and can be applied in all areas of our lives. It's okay to be patient and not feel like you have to rush through life. When you rush, you can miss out on some of the best things. It's okay to not grab the first thing you see all the time. There is a blessing in taking things slow and doing things when you are truly ready, and the good thing is, God knows when you're ready. The Bible says in Proverbs 21:5, "Hasty shortcuts lead to poverty." The Bible discourages hastiness and recklessness. Some things are truly worth the wait.

In my walk with the Lord, I have learned that He is a God of the details, and He doesn't miss a thing when it comes to my life. You see, the devil wants you to be hasty, to make rash decisions, and not pray and walk in the Spirit. He wants you to miss the details. When you rely on God, your spiritual antennas are up and you can discern when something is good or not right. Discernment is a beautiful gift from the Lord.

> **"God proves to be good to the man**
> **who passionately waits,**
> **to the woman who diligently seeks.**
> **It's a good thing to quietly hope,**
> **quietly hope for help from God.**
> **It's a good thing when you're young**
> **to stick it out through the hard times."**
> **(Lamentations 3:25-27, MSG)**

Treasures of Truth

In today's world, where everything is instantly available, we have to learn to be patient and take our time. It takes a long time for a mighty oak to grow from an acorn and the Lord wants us to become oaks of righteousness, a planting of the Lord to display His splendor (Isaiah 61:3), so let patience have its perfect work in you.

Today I Will...

- Pray for the Lord to grant me patience — the fruit of the Holy Spirit.
- Know that I can take my time in becoming who the Lord wants me to be — there is no rush, only the Lord's perfect timing.
- Pray for discernment in all that I do.

Let's Pray...

All-Knowing God, I thank You because I know that You are in control. I will wait on You and I will be still in calmness. I thank You for helping me not to rush ahead of You by using my own wisdom and knowledge instead of Yours. As I read Your Word, I thank You Lord that I will be empowered, strengthened, and full of faith.

In Jesus' Name,

Amen.

DEVOTION 21

God Doesn't have a Plan B!

**"How abundant are the good things
that you have stored up
for those who fear you, that you
bestow in the sight of all,
on those who take refuge in you."
(Psalms 31:19)**

One day, I was walking in the mall and mulling over not being married yet. I said to myself, "I guess I'll just have to cope with it." Then the Holy Spirit spoke to me. He said, *"Why do you have to cope with what is already yours?!"* Powerful, right?

There are things that you have prayed for and are maybe still waiting to manifest in the natural, but the moment you prayed and believed — those things became yours. In Mark 11:24, it says, **"Therefore I tell you, whatever you ask for in prayer, believe that you have received it, and it will be yours."** The Holy Spirit continued to minister to me and let me know that it's already done, and it's already mine! So, rest easy, dear one, God is in control. It is already yours, men and women of God!

Treasures of Truth

God has good things stored up for you in the Spirit. It's only a matter of time for those things to materialize in the natural. He desires to bless you because of who He is.

Today I Will...

- Remember that God has good things stored up for me in the Spirit, and it is only a matter of time for those things to materialize in the natural.

- Believe that God will always answer my prayers — in His time.

Let's Pray...

Heavenly Father, I praise You because I know that You have good plans for my life, and You think good thoughts towards me. I thank You in advance for the wonderful things that You have stored up for me. As I read Your Word and spend time in Your presence, I thank You that I will be strengthened and unwavering in my faith in You.

In Jesus' Name, I pray,

Amen.

DEVOTION 22

Hidden Treasure

**"He has made my mouth like a sharp sword,
In the shadow of His hand He has concealed
Me; And He has also made Me a select
arrow, He has hidden Me in His quiver."
(Isaiah49:2, NASB)**

In the Bible, you will see several times where God hides things of great worth and quality. You may be asking, "Why is God hiding things?" Well, if someone wealthy were to hide something of substance, I would think that there is something very important about this precious item and maybe they don't want the wrong person to get their hands on this valuable item.

Look at Moses. As a baby, he was hidden for three months because of the king's edict. Moses had a great work to do for the Lord and the Lord kept him hidden until the appointed time. You see, God is steps ahead of the enemy, which is why I believe that Scripture to be true that says, "No weapon that is formed against you shall prosper." It can't prosper because God already knows how the weapon is being formed and who is forming the weapon. The devil cannot outsmart God. You are covered by an all-knowing, all-powerful, ever-present, self-sufficient God!

You see, God is protecting you by hiding you because He knows when you will be ready to be seen. He knows when you will be ready to take that platform, that job, that relationship, that opportunity or whatever it is. God knows that you are the man or the woman for the job, just like Moses, and He will protect you and make sure you are ready because He knows what's out there. He knows every plot, scheme, and plan of the enemy, and He not only grooms you for what's ahead when you are hidden but in turn, He protects you too.

**"He will cover you with his feathers.
He will shelter you with his wings.
His faithful promises are your
armor and protection."
(Psalms 91:4, NLT)**

Treasures of Truth

The Bible says in Ecclesiastes 3:1 that to everything, there is a time and a season. There is a time for every purpose under Heaven. Know that God will shelter and protect you — He will hide you until it's the appointed time.

Today I Will...

- Remember that God is hiding me for a great purpose.
- Trust in His plan and know that He will reveal me in His ordained time.
- Enter in the secret place, dwell in His presence, and listen for guidance, direction, and instructions.

Let's Pray...

Heavenly Father, I pray that You would grant me Your revelation and wisdom during this season of being hidden. I pray that the eyes of my heart would be enlightened in order that I may know the hope to which You have called me, and the riches of Your glorious inheritance in Your holy people.

In Jesus' Name,

Amen.

DEVOTION 23

Let God be God!

**"Lord, there is no one like you!
For you are great, and your
name is full of power."
(Jeremiah 10:6, NLT)**

Our journey of faith is not always an easy one. The Bible says that we walk by faith and not by sight. And, in Him, we live and move and have our being. We know that He has planned all our days and has a purpose and plan for us. However, sometimes, this message of walking by faith and dependence on God can get confused by the messages coming from the world that promote independence, self-sufficiency, the visible, and the illusion of control. Messages such as "create your own destiny" or "be in control of your future" or "you can do it if you set your mind to it."

We start to place pressure on ourselves to achieve things the way the world achieves it and to be the way the world wants us to be — this causes us to become overwhelmed with worry, anxiety, and fear. We want to control things but feel totally out of control. As believers, our destiny, our future plans, and our goals are all achieved by God's Spirit in us, not in our own strength.

One day, my heart was feeling so overwhelmed. I poured out my heart to God and told Him my fears and my worries, and He spoke so softly to me. He said four words that calmed my spirit and those words were, *"Let Me Be God."* I repented for worrying, giving in to fear, and trying to have control. God let me know that He was the one controlling everything.

Treasures of Truth

Let God be God in every circumstance of your life. He is the One who is in control and He will work all things out for you. Trust Him. He says to you today:

**"I am the Lord, the God of all the peoples of the world. Is anything too hard for me?"
(Jeremiah 32:27, NLT)**

Today I Will...

- Let go and let God take the lead!
- Not doubt God's ability to take care of me.
- Crucify the flesh and take on the mindset of Christ and stay in faith.

Let's Pray...

Almighty God, I deny my way and take on Your way of doing things. I yield to Your Will for my life and deny myself and take up my cross to follow You. Help me daily as I commit my life to You and crucify my flesh and my old ways of doing things. I place my life in Your hands and trust You every step of the way. In Jesus' Name, I pray,

Amen.

People are Counting on You!

"Therefore, my brothers and sisters, make every effort to confirm your calling and election. For if you do these things, you will never stumble."
(2 Peter 1:10, NIV)

This call is so much bigger than you think. There are literally people waiting on the other side of your obedience. I remember having this dream in college and it still sticks with me to this day.

In the dream, I was with my family in a location and it began to rain. We all had to leave the location because it wasn't safe. I remember deciding to ride home with my aunt and her daughter because she was really scared. I drove with my aunt and told my cousin who was also in the car with us, "I'll be with you through the thick and the thin." I got in the car and my aunt drove to my grandmother's house, where it was a safe place and not raining.

My grandmother lived in the city and on those streets, you have to parallel park to get out of the road. So, I remember my aunt double parking in the middle of the street, getting out of the car, and getting something out of the trunk. She said, "Renee, can you park the car?" I said, "Yes," and got in the driver's seat. I was able to get the car into the parking space. I remember putting the car in park but the car started moving forward on its own. I felt afraid as the car was moving forward because I thought it would hit the car in front of me and, out of fear, I kept pressing the brake to try to stop the car. This happened about three times, and for the third time, not fighting it, I let the car move forward on its own.

Once the car moved forward, it transformed into an extremely fast-moving train, and there were many people on board. The sky was very dark and it was raining heavily in this part of the dream. I remember seeing different nationalities, but the minute I stepped foot in this train, I felt as if I had stepped into my assignment. I had received instructions that I was supposed to stop the train or the people on board would die. I began to feel overwhelmed and asked everyone on the train if they could help me stop the train, but no one offered to help. Then I saw this older man wearing a hat with a large newspaper in his hand, and I thought to myself, "Surely, he will help me." So, I went over to ask the gentleman if he would help me stop the train, and he promised me that he would, but he did not help me.

Then, I just remember this righteous determination rising up on the inside of me, and I asked the Lord to help me figure out how to stop this train. Then the Holy Spirit began to speak to me and He said, *"Go into the part of the train where the conductor sits."* When I walked into that part of the train, I noticed that no one was driving the train, and I happened to look down on the ground and the instructions appeared on the ground. The instructions said to pull the lever, and a red lever appeared and I pulled it. Then the train stopped and the rain stopped. I had an overwhelming feeling of peace that swept over me, and that was the end of the dream.

I believe that dream was very prophetic and I have shared it because there are people that are depending on you to fulfill the assignment and only God can help you complete it successfully.

Treasures of Truth

The call that He places on our lives and the assignments that He gives us, extend way beyond the sphere of our own walk and journey. Like the ripple effect of throwing a stone into calm water — the assignment that God gives you will influence many lives for His Kingdom. Remember that it is only God who can empower you to complete your assignment and influence many lives.

**"But because God was so gracious,
so very generous, here I am.
And I'm not about to let his grace go to waste.
Haven't I worked hard trying to do more than
any of the others? Even then, my work didn't
amount to all that much. <u>It was God giving
me the work to do, God giving me the energy
to do it.</u> So whether you heard it from me or
from those others, it's all the same: We spoke
God's truth and you entrusted your lives."
(1 Corinthians 15:10-11, MSG)**

Today I Will...

- Trust the Lord to empower me with the energy to complete my assignment.
- Know that there are many lives that are dependent on me completing my assignment — keep persevering in my calling.
- Keep praying for His wisdom, strength, and inspiration to complete the calling on my life.

Let's Pray...

Heavenly Father, in my union with Christ Jesus You have created me to live a life of good deeds. These good deeds are an extension of Your work and service to the world through me. Help me to serve with excellence, endurance, and effectiveness as I complete the call that You have on my life to serve others. In Jesus' Name,
Amen.

DEVOTION 25

Those Dreams Shall Live!

"He asked me, 'Son of man,
can these bones live?'
I said, 'Sovereign Lord, you alone know.'
Then he said to me, 'Prophesy to these bones
and say to them, 'Dry bones, hear the word
of the Lord! This is what the Sovereign Lord
says to these bones: I will make breath
enter you, and you will come to life. I will
attach tendons to you and make flesh come
upon you and cover you with skin; I will
put breath in you, and you will come to life.
Then you will know that I am the Lord.'"
(Ezekiel 37:3-6)

A few years ago, I had a dream about giving birth to twins: a boy and a girl. As a matter of fact, I had several dreams about being pregnant with twins.

In this particular dream, I remember living in a small one-bedroom apartment with my babies. I was getting ready for work that day and was rushing, of course, to head out the door. Now, I did something strange, which I would never do in real life. I put both of my babies in brown paper bags and tucked them away in my cupboard drawers. I know that part sounds kind of weird, but the dream is actually very prophetic. So, I tucked the babies away and left for work.

I was gone for a long time. Once I got home, I was extremely worried and hoped the babies hadn't died or suffocated. In distress, I ran over to the drawer took the babies out only to find that they were still alive, but extremely fragile. Out of nowhere, a midwife showed up and helped me nurse my babies. All we did was hold the babies and once they received physical touch, they started getting stronger.

In my dream, I realized that the babies were not normal babies; they were strong and began to grow at an unusually fast rate. Also, the ethnicity of the babies was Mexican, and I am African American, so I know that dream had a spiritual meaning behind it that I'm sure the Lord will continue to reveal to me. The little girl I was holding had hair that started to grow really long and the little boy, who was being held by the midwife, had hair that was very thick, and it started growing too. The little boy was much stronger than the little girl, but I couldn't get to him yet; but we locked eyes and I felt this overwhelming love that swept over me that I couldn't even explain. I was so happy that my babies didn't die.

Just like in my dream, you have some gifts that God has placed on the inside of you and you may have birthed them but placed them to the side or on the back burner — I encourage you to pick them back up. It is not too late. Some dreams, gifts, and desires that God has given you are not dead. Once I touched those babies, they just started to grow naturally on their own. Go back to school, revisit that business plan, start developing that plan for the school you want to open, and get to work. Watch it grow and blossom into what God has ordained. The world needs what you have — so work it.

"So I prophesied as I was commanded. And as I was prophesying, there was a noise, a rattling sound, and the bones came together, bone to bone. I looked, and tendons and flesh appeared on them and skin covered them, but there was no breath in them."

"Then he said to me, 'Prophesy to the breath; prophesy, son of man, and say to it, 'This is what the Sovereign Lord says: Come, breath, from the four winds and breathe into these slain, that they may live.' So I prophesied as he commanded me, and breath entered them; they came to life and stood up on their feet—a vast army."
(Ezekiel 37:7-10)

I had another dream where I was in this house with my baby, a little boy this time. This other little boy in a black hoodie was trying to get into my house. He kept throwing things at the window and literally shaking the door to try and pull it open. I remember at one point of the dream, he opened the door and threw a rock at my baby and hit him, and he started crying. At that point, it was a wrap for him! I stood in front of my baby so he couldn't get near him and drove him out of my house — and he never returned.

The enemy is threatened by that which you are carrying on the inside of you. You see, God hides treasures and gifts on the inside of man. What God has birthed in you, the devil wants to kill because it is so great, but I am here to tell you that you have the authority to drive out evil spirits. They have no place in your home or near your gifting, purposes, dreams, and desires. Protect what God has given you.

"I have given you authority to trample on snakes and scorpions and to overcome all the power of the enemy; nothing will harm you."
(Luke 10:19)

Treasures of Truth

The gifting and dreams that the Lord has placed within you will come to life as you start exercising them. If you put some things on the back-burner that God told you to do, pick them back up — it's not too late. Allow God to bring those gifts and visions to life.

Today I Will...

- Pick up the forgotten dreams and ask the Holy Spirit for the strength and courage to begin again.
- I will not believe the negative voices and thoughts that tell me it's too late to fulfill my dreams.
- Be intentional about birthing the dreams God has placed on the inside of me. I will realize how important these dreams are and ask God to help me put together a game plan or a list of goals on how to birth these dreams.

Let's Pray...

Heavenly Father, I thank You for entrusting me with such precious dreams and purpose. I am excited about the dreams You have birthed in me, and how the world will be blessed by what You've placed on the inside of me. I thank You, that I will be anxious for nothing and will lean on You each step of the way.

In Jesus' Name,

Amen.

Struggling with Lust?

**"Flee the evil desires of youth
and pursue righteousness,
faith, love and peace,
along with those who call on the Lord
out of a pure heart."
(2 Timothy 2:22)**

One day, this Scripture rang so loudly in my ears, "Satan comes to steal, kill, and destroy." We cannot play around with the devil — even if he appears as 'good' or he offers us 'love' — he wants to steal, kill, and destroy you.

If you are struggling with lust, give it to God! Let me tell you, the temptation is real but let's choose to be like Joseph and flee out of every situation that is not right.

**"She caught him by his cloak
and said, 'Come to bed with me!'
But he left his cloak in her hand
and ran out of the house."
(Genesis 39:12)**

You cannot play with fire. Remember what the Lord promises in His Word:

"So, if you think you are standing firm,
be careful that you don't fall!
No temptation has overtaken you
except what is common to mankind.
And God is faithful;
he will not let you be tempted
beyond what you can bear.
But when you are tempted,
he will also provide a way out
so that you can endure it."
(1 Corinthians 10: 12-13)

Before Joseph was promoted, he had to be tested and God allowed it. Joseph qualified himself for the blessing because he did not compromise.

"Blessed is the one who perseveres under
trial because, having stood the test, that
person will receive the crown of life that the
Lord has promised to those who love him."
(James 1:12-13)

Treasures of Truth

Sometimes, temptation can feel like a flood that comes rushing in. We think that we will be overwhelmed and that we can't stand up under it. During those times, run towards God and cling to Him. Cry out to Him to deliver you. He promises that He will not allow you to be tempted beyond your ability to endure and rest in that assurance. He will always make a way of escape.

**"Submit yourselves, then, to God.
Resist the devil, and he will flee from you."
(James 4:7)**

Today I Will...

- Run towards God when I am tempted — not away from Him.
- Cling to Him and seek the way of escape!
- Not allow any doors to be opened in my life that gives the devil access.
- I will guard my heart and mind. I will keep my mind on things that are pure and pleasing to the Lord.

Let's Pray...

Almighty God, I thank You for Your overcoming grace and strength to overcome lust. I thank You for always providing a way of escape and not allowing me to be tempted above what I can bear. As I think on those things that are pure and lovely, strengthen me, God. I thank you for helping me to stand firm in my integrity and walk in purity to please You.

In the Precious Name of Jesus,
Amen.

DEVOTION 27

You Just Wait and See

"But as it is written:
"Eye has not seen, nor ear heard,
Nor have entered into the heart of man
The things which God has prepared
for those who love Him."
(1 Corinthians 2:9, NKJV)

What God does in your life is going to be beyond what you could ever think! One day, I was sitting on the couch in my parents' living room and I heard God speak to me inside. He said, *"Renee, do you trust me?"* I replied back and said, "Yes, I trust You, Lord," and I meant it with all my heart. Then I heard Him say with such confidence and exhilaration, *"You just wait and see!"* I could feel the strength and passionate zeal in His voice and my heart became overjoyed. God wants us to trust Him. Do you understand the magnitude of this? God wants to show Himself to be strong in your life, so trust in Him.

"But blessed is the man who trusts me, God,
the woman who sticks with God.
They're like trees replanted in Eden,
putting down roots near the rivers—
Never a worry through the hottest of
summers,
never dropping a leaf,
Serene and calm through droughts,
bearing fresh fruit every season.
(Jeremiah 17:7-8, MSG)

Treasures of Truth

God can do way beyond we can ever hope or imagine. Trust Him.

**"Oh, the depth of the riches of the wisdom
and knowledge of God!
How unsearchable his judgments,
and his paths beyond tracing out!
"Who has known the mind of the Lord?
Or who has been his counselor?"
"Who has ever given to God,
that God should repay them?"
For from him and through him
and for him are all things.
To him be the glory forever! Amen."
(Romans 11:33-36)**

Today I Will...

- Hope in God with an expectant heart, because I realize that He opens doors that no man can shut and He shuts doors that no man can open.
- Know that God has wonderful things in store for me — way beyond what I could hope or imagine.

Let's Pray...

Almighty God, I thank You because You can go beyond what I could ever imagine or think. There are no limits for You! I will be still and know that You are God. Strengthen me as I keep my eyes on You. I thank You because You have good plans for my life and to give me the future that I am hoping for.

In Jesus' Name,

Amen.

DEVOTION 28

Ask for BIG Things

**"Now to Him who is able to do
exceedingly abundantly
above all that we ask or think,
according to the power that works in us,
to Him be glory in the church by Christ Jesus
to all generations,
forever and ever.
Amen."
(Ephesians 3:20-21)**

One day, on my train ride home, the Lord began to speak to me. He shared with me how He wired and framed me. He said, *"Renee, you are an astute woman; an astute leader. I made you that way."* Then He said, *"Since you have honored me with your life, I will honor you with my favor."* He told me that He created everything and it all came from His hands. He then said, *"Renee, ask of Me what you will."* and when I started speaking, He said, *"Renee ask for BIG THINGS because I am a big God."* I remember driving in the car one day and talking to the Lord. I shared with Him what I wanted to do with my life. I first said, "I want to sell makeup," then I went on to say, "No, I want to start a makeup line." Then I said, "Actually, I want to build an empire." Then I heard God speak, and He said, *"Now, you're thinking on my level."*

"For My thoughts *are* not your thoughts,
Nor *are* your ways My ways," says the Lord.
"For *as* the heavens are higher than the earth,
So are My ways higher than your ways,
And My thoughts than your thoughts."
(Isaiah 55:8-9)

Treasures of Truth

Sometimes, in our humanness, we tend to place our limitations on God. We think within the limits of time, space, and our own ideas of possibility. But God is way beyond the limits that we place on ourselves and on Him — He is a BIG GOD!

"But He said, 'The things which are impossible with men are possible with God.'"
(Luke 18:27, NKJV)

Today I Will...

- Not put God in a box and will expect big things that go beyond my dreams, hopes, and desires.
- Trust in my BIG God to do Mighty things.

Let's Pray...

Heavenly Father, I thank You because I can come to You confidently and boldly before Your throne of grace. I thank You for going above and beyond I could ever hope for. I thank You for doing the impossible in my life so that everyone will know it was You. Thank You for the great things You have planned and already made ready for me.

In Jesus' Name,

Amen.

DEVOTION 29

God is the Source!

**"Both riches and honor *come* from You,
And You reign over all.
In Your hand *is* power and might;
In Your hand *it is* to make great
And to give strength to all."
(1 Chronicles 29:12, NKJV)**

I remember getting ready to graduate with my undergraduate degree from ORU and I had a hard time finding a work-study or job that semester, and funds were very tight. I needed $50 to purchase a cap and gown to walk across the stage, and I didn't have the money. I was so used to running to my parents and asking them for funds but they didn't have it, so I felt stuck. I didn't want to ask anyone because I felt embarrassed and didn't want anyone to think, "Wow, she doesn't even have $50!"

For some reason, I went to the university bookstore and noticed that they were doing a prize giveaway and were collecting raffle tickets to win one of a few prizes. So, I bought a ticket but thought to myself, "You never win any of these games!" But I still prayed over the ticket and went my way.

Out of the three gifts, you could win a free cap and gown which was awesome! So, after putting in my raffle ticket, I went back to my room and I just went to sleep. For some reason, I said to myself, "I'm not going to keep stressing about this cap and gown anymore." And let me tell you, while I was asleep, God was working!

Now that is a Word for some of you reading this right now.

When I woke up, I had a voicemail and several texts on my phone from friends. I found out that I was one of the winners for the free giveaways. And can you guess what prize I won?! The cap and gown!! God is so good!

I will never forget one girl asked me if we could trade because she had won a picture frame and I said, "No, I'm sorry." I needed that cap and gown because I didn't have the money to pay for it at the time. God is so faithful!

"Look at the birds of the air, that they do not sow, nor reap nor gather into barns, and yet your heavenly Father feeds them. Are you not worth much more than they?"
(Matthew 6:26, NKJV)

Treasures of Truth

When God says that He will provide *all* your needs, He means *all your needs*. Know that He is your Provider and the One who cares for you. He is your source. Also, remember, when God blesses you with something, be careful not to "give" our blessings away just because you feel you have to be "nice" as a Christian.

Today I Will...

- Trust in my Provider to care for *all* my needs.
- Anticipate blessings from the Lord and have a heart of expectancy.

Let's Pray...

Heavenly Father, I thank You that You supply all of my needs and everything that I need comes from You. You are the source of everything and I thank You for always taking care of me. Always cause me to be at the right place at the right time and cause opportunities to open up all around me.

In Jesus' Name,

Amen.

DEVOTION 30

You Will be Envied!

**"You prepare a table before me
in the presence of my enemies;
You anoint my head with oil;
My cup runs over."
(Psalm 23:5, NKJV)**

Do you feel surrounded by enemies and haters?
Then you are in the right place — and I'll tell you
why. Have you ever felt like all eyes were on you and
people looked at you and despised you? It might be
the people close to you, people at your work, or
people anywhere. These people want to see you
fail, but I have a word for you: the haters and the
enemies are right on queue. King David realized
this in the book of Psalms when he said that the
Lord prepared a table before him in the presence
of his enemies, anointed his head with oil, and his
cup overflowed with blessings. Be encouraged,
because God is giving your enemies a front row
seat to your blessings!

You see, I've come to find that the people who gossip about someone or conspire against that person; their plans always backfire, and God seemed to always bless the very one that they were talking about. I believe that God does this on purpose. It's His endorsement of your life. It's like He says, *"I don't care who doesn't like you, I'll show the world how much I love you through My favor even if they hate you. Their hate isn't greater than my love!"*

I've personally experienced envy from others. When I was placed in positions of leadership and appointment, there were people that despised and hated me. I found that those people always wanted to find out what I was doing so they could compete and try to outdo me. However, when you are anointed by God to do something, whoever copies, they cannot do it like you! The sad part is that those people do not know who they are or that they have an assignment from God. They are using all their energy and strength to focus on you — and not God. Pray for them, seriously.

For a long time, I used to get so angry with those people and a lot of my energy went towards caring about their actions until the Lord gave me a heart-to-heart one day on my lunch break. He said,

"Renee, you are getting distracted. You are getting angry with these people, and not focusing on what I told you to do. This is serious and bigger than you. Let Me deal with them, but you continue doing what I told you to do. People need to hear what you have to say, and this is serious. You are expending a lot of your energy on these people when it needs to be saved for the real purpose, for the people I need you to reach." See, Satan is behind all of this and just wants to create distractions, so that you cannot operate at your maximum level of creativity and anointing. There was a time where it used to hurt me deeply knowing that people didn't like me. I just wanted to crawl under a rock and not to be great so that I wouldn't offend anyone; but having that mindset, in all actuality, was offending God. The Lord swiftly reminded me that I had a choice to make. Was I going to allow the opinions of others to stop me from fulfilling the work that He wanted me to do? Or would I press on? Would I press past the jealousy, envy, and competitive spirits? He reminded me that this was bigger than the people that didn't like me. People will not like it when the Lord elevates and promotes you but know that the Lord is for you. You are destined for greatness and designed to do great things, always remember that!

"Am I now trying to win the approval of human beings, or of God? Or am I trying to please people? If I were still trying to please people, I would not be a servant of Christ."
(Galatians 1:10)

Looking back, I can definitely see how God prepared me for the level of envy and jealousy I would face on my new job. Just like David fought the lion and the bear, we do the same in our training in order to be ready for Goliath. I am just warning you now that you will encounter jealousy and envy — and on different levels, but I am here to tell you that you *can* handle it because the greater one lives on the inside of you.

"You are of God, little children,
and have overcome them,
because He who is in you is greater
than he who is in the world."
(1 John 4:4, NKJV)

I read this quote and it said, "Sometimes things don't get easier, you just get better." And what came to my mind is you are being made. God is allowing or using this to make you!

Treasures of Truth

God allows these situations to mold and make you. He uses them to refine you so that you come out stronger. If you are facing a situation today where you encounter envy or jealousy, bring that situation to God and Trust Him to give you the courage to keep serving Him with a spirit of excellence.

Today I Will...

- Know that with God on my side — we are the majority.
- Know that I will be fine even if no one likes me because God is with me and loves me.
- Pray for wisdom on how to handle every situation where I may encounter jealousy or envy.

Let's Pray...

Heavenly Father, I thank You that Your favor surrounds me like a shield. No weapon that is formed against me shall prosper. As I keep a pure and humble heart, I ask that You expose the enemy's plans and cause them to become null and void. Thank You for protecting me and causing all things to work together for my good.

In Jesus' Name,

Amen.

DEVOTION 31

Angelic Reinforcements

**"The angel of the LORD encamps around those who fear Him, And rescues them."
(Psalm 34:7)**

At 19 years old, I had an encounter with two angels when I was dating this guy that I met in college. But before I tell you about that encounter, let me give you some background.

After the whole bullying situation, my parents took my brother and me out of public school and placed us into a small local private school in the suburbs. In my graduating senior class, there were only three guys, so when I got to college I was really eager to start dating. Remember earlier in this book, I shared with you that I wanted to attend Oral Roberts University, but was not accepted the first time so I had to attend community college my first year right after high school? Now, I wanted to remind you about this because you will see why angels became involved in this particular time of my life. I ended up meeting this young man at the community college right before I was planning to transition into Oral Roberts University.

Now, this young man did not have good intentions and kept on pressuring me to have sex with him on our dates. (Now, I'm not saying that I was perfect all the way. I did entertain kissing this guy and you shouldn't be passionately kissing a man or woman unless it's your spouse). Well, back to my angelic encounter. On our first date, we ended up going to the mall because we didn't have a lot of money. We walked around, talked, and decided to eat in the food court. We were sitting and eating when I noticed two men walk towards us. One man was Black and the other was White. The Black man was watching me and looked very concerned, and the White man watched my date. The Black man gave me a lingering look of concern and I felt as if I shouldn't have been on the date with this young man. My date then got up from the table and said, "I'll be right back, I'm going to get some more rice from the Chinese booth," and I said okay.

When he got up, I noticed the White gentleman also got up and he just stood near my date in front of the Chinese booth. Then the Black man got up and walked and stood right next to me and didn't say a word. I looked up and he was just standing there, watching me and didn't say a word. I was a bit creeped out by this and when my date got back to the table I asked him, "Did you know those men? They kept on watching us. Did you see what the Black man did?" And his response back was, "What men?"

We left the food court and got into his car. It was a beautiful sunny day; gorgeous weather. In the car, my date started flirting with me and then asked if he could have a kiss on the cheek, and I said yes. He then asked for a kiss on the lips, so we started kissing. Then, he wanted to take it further with the kissing and I didn't feel right about doing it. While we were kissing, the sunroof was open and a drop of rain hit him hard in the face. We both looked up to the sky and noticed that the sky turned dark, and the clouds were dark gray. It started to rain suddenly with thunder and it kind of scared me. The wind started blowing so hard that the car began to rock from side to side, and my date said, "I should probably get you home." Once we left the mall and started heading to my parents, the sky immediately cleared and the sun began to shine brightly, just as if it never rained.

On one of our last dates, we were sitting in the car in the Farmer's Market parking lot. We were listening to jazz music and eating ice cream. However, things got bad again and we began doing a lot of kissing. I just remember looking up to see not one, but two police cars on both sides of our car. I did not hear these cars pull up nor did I hear any noise — I just saw the lights. I said to my date, "Look, the cops are here, we should go." So, we left.

All night long, this young man wanted to have sex and I shouldn't have entertained it, but I liked him so much. After one last attempt to get me to compromise, he said, "It's okay if we have sex. God can make you a virgin again." Right at that moment, I knew that that was all he wanted from me. If I would have entertained this young man's proposition, I would have possibly fallen pregnant and messed up my chances of getting into ORU that coming fall semester.

After he dropped me off home that night, I didn't hear from him for a whole month. He dropped me like a hot potato and I was so glad that I didn't give my purity away. If anyone is pressuring you into having sex before marriage, that is not the one that God has for you. The man or woman that God gives you is going to want to honor God in this area of their life, as well as encourage you to stay strong in your purity walk. God knows the intents of a person's heart and just like at thirteen, He stepped in and brought angelic assistance to help me not make a big mistake and experience a huge heartbreak. Thank you, Jesus!!!

Treasures of Truth

God will send angelic reinforcement to keep you on track. He will not allow you to forfeit your destiny on things that aren't worth it.

**"To him who is able to keep you
from stumbling and to present you
before his glorious presence without
fault and with great joy—
to the only God our Savior
be glory, majesty, power and
authority, through Jesus Christ
our Lord, before all ages,
now and forevermore! Amen."
(Jude 24-25)**

Today I Will...

- Pray that He commands His angels to guard me in all my ways.
- Trust Him to send help when I need it.
- Know that He is able to keep me from falling and to present me faultless before Him.

Let's Pray...

All-knowing Father, thank You for sending angelic reinforcements to protect and rescue me. I thank you, Lord, that there are more with me than there are against me. Help me to be aware of the presence of angels and remember that You are protecting me on every side.

In Jesus' Name,

Amen.

DEVOTION 32

Angels in High Places

**"For he will command his
angels concerning you
to guard you in all your ways."
(Psalms 91:11)**

I remember starting a new job and God telling me, *"Renee, when you stepped foot in this place, you brought Me with you and there are going to be some changes."* The very next week, my boss told me that there were changes taking place and that I had been moved to work with another group. This was truly the favor of God. Ever since God told me that I brought Him with me, I began to feel the tangible presence of angels in front of my desk.

One particular day, I felt all the hairs on body standing up and I had goosebumps on my arms — I could sense a presence. The night before, I had felt the very same presence in my room and I had felt afraid but I knew that it was an angel. This angel felt extremely huge and I sensed that he filled up the entire room with how big he was. I felt as if I was covered by this huge angel. So, I was sitting at my desk wondering if anyone else could feel what I was feeling and of course, they could not. I just knew an archangel was there with me. He was standing directly in front of my desk, watching me. I felt like Daniel when he first saw Michael. He was terrified and fell on his face. I had goosebumps running up and down my arms. I could feel this huge presence, and I knew it was very strong. I couldn't even concentrate while I was at my desk. I felt as if I was going to burst out and pray in the Spirit really loudly. I had to immediately get up and go to the bathroom. I felt like crying but not in a scary way. A war cry was welling deep within my belly. I knew it was time for war — war in the Spirit.

Now, before this encounter, I was definitely aware of the presence of angels and when they got close to me, the hairs on my neck would stand up, but this time, the hairs on my entire body stood up! When I returned to my desk, I could feel him hovering over me and it lasted for over thirty minutes. He came with me into the office and God reminded me of what He told me when I first started working there: *"When you stepped foot in this place, you brought Me with you."*

You see, when God takes you up to high places, He will sometimes send His high-ranking angels to combat those principalities, powers, and the wickedness in those places.

Treasures of Truth

"Then I looked and heard the voice of many angels, numbering thousands upon thousands, and ten thousand times ten thousand. They encircled the throne and the living creatures and the elders."
(Revelation 5:11)

Just like Elijah saw in the Spirit regarding the number of angels that were fighting with him, we must remember that there are more with us than against us.

Today I Will...

- Remember that the Lord of Hosts goes with me wherever I go.
- Know that He will send his angels to war on my behalf.

Let's Pray...

Heavenly Father, I thank You for releasing Your warring and high-ranking angels to go into new territories with me that You have assigned. I ask that they contend on my behalf and prevail against the principalities and spiritual wickedness in high places. Thank You for Your power and angelic reinforcements.

In Jesus' Name,
Amen.

DEVOTION 33

Keep Moving Forward

**"Jesus replied, 'No one who puts a hand
to the plow and looks back is fit for
service in the kingdom of God.'"**
(Luke 9:62)

Are you feeling tempted to go backward? A while
ago, I felt tempted to go back into an unhealthy
relationship and job. The Lord used the following
incident to teach me a valuable lesson.

One day, I was driving in an unfamiliar area
and was trying to exit the parking lot. Now, at
one particular spot, I had to reverse the car and
I checked my rearview mirror to see if there was
anything behind me. I saw a concrete island in the
mirror. It looked like the island was far away, so I
began to back up the car and didn't pay attention to
what I was doing. Suddenly, I heard and felt a large
bump. I had hit the concrete island in the middle
of the road. I got out of the car and checked the
bumper only to find a small dent in the back of my

car, and then I heard the Holy Spirit speak to me. He said, *"Good thing it was only a small dent and the entire car didn't get damaged."* Then He said, *"Isn't this like life? Renee, just like you didn't realize that the concrete was that close, Satan has traps set up for you that you are unaware of if you go back to that relationship."* He went on to say that the choice was mine, but that He wanted me to choose His best. He also said, *"Don't ever go back in your relationships, your jobs, or in life — keep going forward."*

That is the word for you today, *"FORWARD."*

Treasures of Truth:

It is not God's will for us to stay in dysfunctional relationships or to go back to them. The blessing of the Lord will make you rich and won't add any type of sorrow to your life. Don't go back to ungodly relationships or places because you feel alone or comfortable with what was but press into what God has for you. *Keep moving forward!*

"Brethren, I count not myself to have apprehended: but this one thing I do, forgetting those things which are behind, and reaching forth unto those things which are before,"
(Philippians 3:13, KJV)

Today I Will...

- Keep moving forward.
- Not allow myself to dwell on my past — but to know that God has the future all set out.

Let's Pray...

Heavenly Father, I thank You because You are good and You always sustain me. As I move forward and obey Your voice, I ask that You would grant me courage and strength. I thank You, Lord, that Your purposes will always prevail in my life. I ask You, Lord, that You would help me with my emotions. As I walk in the Spirit and not in the flesh, I thank You for increasing my strength and agility. I will press toward the mark for the prize of the high calling in Christ Jesus.

In the Mighty Name of Jesus,
Amen.

DEVOTION 34

Conversations with God

"God, your God, will restore everything you lost; he'll have compassion on you; he'll come back and pick up the pieces from all the places where you were scattered." (Deuteronomy 30:3-5, MSG)

Looking back on my dating experiences, I remember God kept echoing the same theme to me over and over again. He wanted me to know my value and worth, and not to settle for anything less. I went through a season where God did not want me to date, and He wanted me to be still to hear His voice and allow Him to build me up and build up my esteem where it had been knocked down from bullying and rejection. However, I was proud and did not want to work on my heart. I wanted to date and do what *I* wanted which caused me to settle over and over again in wrong relationships.

When we don't listen to God or focus on what He wants us to focus on, it causes unnecessary heartbreaks and sometimes causes us to waste time in these relationships. However, through all of this, God did not give up on me. He kept speaking and when I would ask Him if I could date certain guys, He would always say *"No."* I used to feel as if God liked telling me "no" and I didn't understand it at the time. But now, I realize it was Him respecting the worth that He created in me by not endorsing me to be with the wrong guys — now that's love!

I remember sitting in my car one day and asking God to put me in a relationship with this one guy that I really liked. I cried out to God and told Him that I was lonely and wanted a companion. I heard Him say with such authority in His voice, *"No, Renee. I'm not going to do it. I'm not going to jip you like that. I'm not going to give you less than the best."* Wow, what a conversation to have with God! He went on to say that the young man was not ready and that I needed to pray for him. He gave me a stern *"No"*. God will protect your worth even when you don't or can't see it at the time.

Even after this powerful conversation with God, I still didn't get it and pursued further relationships that I had no business being in. One day, God spoke to me and it finally clicked. I was with this guy and he did not value and respect me. The relationship was all about him, and even though I wasn't happy in this relationship, I still put him before myself. That day, while I was in the kitchen, the Lord spoke to me and He said, *"Renee, why do you keep putting yourself last?! Why? You matter!"* Then the Holy Spirit started connecting the dots for me and showed me how, in times before, I kept doing the same thing. I finally learned the lesson that God wanted me to get. I began to go through the healing process and gain a healthy esteem within myself.

Now, after this relationship had ended, I hid in the secret place with God. I clung to Him, like a little kid that hangs on to his or her father's leg. I stayed close to the Father and He began to build me up. I remember, there were times when I would go into His presence feeling empty and come out feeling like a million bucks! He let me know that I was strong, beautiful, powerful, smart, and most of all valued. In those moments, I received God's blessing and endorsement in my life.

Treasures of Truth

Struggling with low self-esteem? Allow God to build you up and tell you who you really are. Trust me, you'll never be the same. If you are feeling sad or depressed because that relationship didn't work out, please know that it may not have been God's best for you. Be discerning and sensitive to the Holy Spirit's leading and use this time to allow God to work on your heart like a surgeon. Let Him go in and work on the deep things and deep hurts that no one knows about. Open your heart to Him and let Him do a work in you. Realize that, you have value and worth, and don't just settle for any guy or any girl, because you are:

"... a chosen people, a royal priesthood, a holy nation, God's special possession, that you may declare the praises of him who called you out of darkness into his wonderful light."
(1 Peter 2:9)

So, get up, fix yourself up, square those shoulders back and walk with your head held high, because you are a strong force within this earth and a power house because of God's Spirit that is within you!

Today I Will...

- Know that I have value and worth — I've been bought with the precious blood of Jesus.

- Let God do His internal work in me and make me whole.
- Meditate on the truth that Abba Father knows what is best for my life. He knows all the pieces of the puzzle, and I can rest in the fact that God knows who to add to my life. Even when I don't understand, I will trust in knowing that the Lord has better in store for me.

Let's Pray...

Loving Father, as I enter into Your chambers, I open my heart to You. Fill me up with all of You! Thank you for being a safe haven for my emotions, struggles, hurts, and innermost thoughts. Your presence is so refreshing! As I dwell in Your secret place, cause me to be better than I was before I came in. Deepen the hunger in my heart for You, so that I crave Your presence every day. As the deer pants for streams of water, so my soul pants for You, Lord. Thank You for strengthening my heart and aligning it with Yours.

In Jesus' Name,

Amen.

DEVOTION 35

God Will Awaken Your Spiritual Senses

**"Wherefore he saith, Awake thou that sleepest, and arise from the dead, and Christ shall give thee light."
(Ephesians 5:14, KJV)**

As you are growing in God, the Holy Spirit will help you to become sensitive to Him and see things in the Spirit. I am still growing in God, as we all are, and He is training my spiritual eyes to be able to see things that are going on in the supernatural.

Recently, while on my way home, I had to wait for the metro. I sat on a two-sided bench and I was the only one sitting on my side. However, on the side behind me, there were three gentlemen sitting, waiting for the metro on their side. All of a sudden, this guy arrived. He had long dreads and was wearing a black hoodie. He sat right between these men and directly behind me. I noticed that he was playing this loud music from his phone which sounded like rap music, but to me, it sounded very demonic and I felt a presence that didn't feel right. I looked back and noticed that none of the men sitting next to him happened to look up or ask him to turn his music down, and I thought to myself, wow, maybe they don't see him. Then, at that moment, I spoke out of my mouth, "I plead the Blood of Jesus" and the music went away. Then, I looked around the metro station and could not find the guy in the black hoodie. Also, the Holy Spirit brought to my mind, *"Did you notice that he didn't sit on your side of the bench? There was plenty of space. It's because the demons also recognize the blood of Jesus that is in you!"* Use your spiritual authority, young men and women of God.

Pay attention to what is going on inside of your spirit, because God is developing your spiritual senses and awareness. In the Spirit, things move fast. I have experienced this when in that sleepy state just before falling asleep. I could hear a lot of noise and it felt as if things were moving very quickly and there are many things going on. Allow the Lord to take you beyond the natural realm and always remember that there is more than what you can see on the surface.

The Lord kept building my spiritual awareness and would allow me to feel things in my spirit on several occasions. I took a trip with a friend to Cancun, Mexico and it was awesome! We enjoyed our time and explored the culture, food, and the people. However, I will never forget when we went to visit a historic area considered as one of the Seven Wonders of the World. We ended up going on a guided tour. At a certain arena, I could sense a demonic presence. Our tour guide explained that in this particular area, there was an actual combat amongst the people and it was a barbaric fighting. I could feel a ringing in my ears, almost like static. I felt like there were giant principalities in the area and I had to step away and cover my ears. I began to plead the Blood of Jesus over myself. My friend did not understand what was going on and asked if I was okay, and we ended up having to leave that place. The supernatural is very real.

I kept experiencing these encounters over and over again. I could mention several encounters that I've had — from driving through a back road in the North East past a cotton field and feeling such a strong demonic spirit of oppression in the atmosphere to working at the Prayer Tower at ORU (a telephone counseling ministry) and receiving a call from a demon-possessed woman. She began to scream on the phone and I could feel like a shock of electricity in my ears, and it sounded like a static noise. It got so strong, I had to take my headset off, end the call, and pray. You will have so many encounters with angels and the supernatural, but I believe that God will show you these things when He knows that you are ready.

God can use His angels to help you in your everyday life, even to wake you up in time to prepare for a presentation in college, which is what happened to me. A couple of my friends and I would stay up very late, working on papers and homework while watching movies and hanging out. One night, we stayed up till about 5:00 am cranking out papers, and then I headed back to my room to get some rest. I needed to wake up by 8:00 am to head to the library and prepare for a presentation for my Strategic Management class. This class was the capstone course that I needed to pass in order to obtain my master's degree. Before setting my alarm, I must have been half asleep or really out of it, because I set my alarm for the wrong time. It was set for 8:00 pm instead of 8:00 am. Now, my roommate at the time was a nursing student and she had clinicals at 6:00 am and was normally gone by the time I had to wake up. While I was asleep, I could feel someone vigorously shaking me to wake me up, and then I woke up. I looked at the time and realized that I was just in time to head to the library to complete my PowerPoint presentation. I noticed that my roommate was gone and went to check the door and found that the door was locked. It kind of scared me because I said to myself, "Renee, who shook you to wake you up?" Then I realized that it was God's angels. God will send angelic assistance to help you in college life, the workforce or wherever you may need help.

Treasures of Truth

The spiritual realm is real. God will reveal it to you in His timing. He alone knows when you are ready to grow in spiritual discernment, so once more, trust in His process.

**"The Son is the image of the invisible God, the firstborn over all creation. For in him all things were created: things in heaven and on earth, visible and invisible, whether thrones or powers or rulers or authorities; all things have been created through him and for him. He is before all things, and in him all things hold together."
(Colossians 1:15-17)**

Today I Will...

- Be intentionally aware that things are going on in the Spirit.
- Ask the Lord to help me to be aware and to open my spiritual eyes to see.

Let's Pray

Gracious God, I ask that You would grant me wisdom on how to activate my spiritual senses. As I set aside time in Your presence, teach me how to discern in the Spirit and go beyond what is in the natural realm. Teach me Your ways God and train my spiritual eyes to see and ears to hear in the Spirit very accurately. Pour and download Your revelation into my Spirit.

In Jesus' Name,

Amen.

DEVOTION 36

Mantles of Intercession

**"Pray at all times in the Spirit with
every prayer and request,
and stay alert in this with all
perseverance and intercession
for all the saints."
(Ephesians 6:18, HCSB)**

The Lord will prompt you to pray for others. One day, I remember driving through Chick-fil-A and ordering food. I could sense a spirit of depression on the young man at the drive-thru window and I felt an urgency to pray immediately. I prayed for this young man for two days and then I felt a release. On another occasion, on the way to work, I saw a little girl at the bus stop and felt the need to pray for her. I felt as if she felt stuck and was prompted inside to immediately begin to pray for her and pray against generational curses in her family. I could sense that God was going to allow her to be the first to do great things in her family and that she's a bloodline curse breaker.

The first time I encountered these promptings to pray intensely for others was during the Bible study at work. At that time, one of my spiritual leaders had recently come back from Salvador and shared pictures from her trip with the group. In the picture, there were young girls who came from very poor areas and the two leaders would constantly sow into a ministry that helps these young girls. They asked us to pray as we felt led and I just remember sitting there, listening to others pray and then this deep feeling came over me. I could feel the girls' despair in the picture and began to weep. I could not control it. I felt compassion and a strong spirit of intercession came over me at that moment. I remember just crying uncontrollably and then one of the leaders said, "You have a burden and you need to let it out." Then I began to pray for those girls in the picture and felt an immediate release.

The Lord was developing this gift in me and He led me to pray and intercede for longer periods of time. I remember constantly talking to God about an old friend from school and He said, *"Renee, I want you to pray for him. Stand in the gap for him."* I prayed for this young man for about five years. Every time he would come to my mind, I would immediately pray for him. During that time, God confirmed to me that He did indeed want me to pray and intercede for this friend. I hadn't told anyone that I was praying for him and sometimes, after praying, I would feel physically tired in my body. After one of the Bible study sessions at work, one of the prophets came up to me and said, "You are carrying someone in the Spirit. It's like you sleep for hours but you still feel tired." He then encouraged me to keep praying for my friend and I was blown away by this encounter. On the day when my assignment to intercede for this friend finished, I was in my apartment with another friend praying for him. Then during the prayer, I felt a warmth and peace deep in my spirit. I could sense a release and a feeling that my prayers had prevailed. It was amazing!

**"Ask of me, and I will make the
nations your heritage,
and the ends of the earth your possession."
(Psalms 2:8)**

Treasures of Truth

There are mantles of intercession that the Lord will release upon you. Pay attention to the promptings to pray and intercede for those that the Lord brings to your mind.

**"In the same way, the Spirit helps us in our weakness. We do not know what we ought to pray for, but the Spirit himself intercedes for us through wordless groans. And he who searches our hearts knows the mind of the Spirit, because the Spirit intercedes for God's people in accordance with the will of God."
(Romans 8:26-27)**

Today I Will...

- Allow the Lord to develop the gift of intercession in me.
- Pray when I feel a prompting to pray — let me be obedient to the Holy Spirit within.

Let's Pray...

Heavenly Father, I thank You for the power of prayer. I know that the prayers of the righteous have much power. As I remain sensitive to the Holy Spirit, guide me on who to pray for and what to pray. As a watchman on the wall, give me Your wisdom and strategic prayers to pray. Fuel the fire in my heart for prayer. Use me and allow me to be one of Your people to build up the wall and stand in the gap on behalf of the land.

In Jesus' Name,

Amen.

DEVOTION 37

Visions

**"'In the last days, God says,
I will pour out my Spirit on all people.
Your sons and daughters will prophesy,
your young men will see visions,
your old men will dream dreams.'"
(Acts 2:17)**

While attending Oral Roberts University, God began to awaken my spiritual senses in the area of visions. One particular time, after class, I returned to my dorm room and lay down in my bed. My eyes were closed but I was not asleep. While my eyes were closed, I could see myself in this vision and there was this bright light shining on my face. The light was so bright, and it was as if Heaven had its attention on me!

Then the Lord revealed to me what that meant. I had a daily devotional calendar in my room and for some reason, I happened to look at it after I had that vision. The devotion for that day had 2

Corinthians 3:17-18 (MSG) listed and after reading, it kind of shook me up. I thought, "Wow, God is really confirming Himself." The Scripture said:

**"God is a living, personal presence...
And when God is personally present,
a living spirit, that old, constricting
legislation is recognized as obsolete...
Nothing between us and God,
our FACES shining
with the BRIGHTNESS of his face, and
so we are transfigured much like the
Messiah, our lives gradually becoming
brighter and more beautiful as God enters
our lives and we become like him."**

This Scripture confirmed exactly what happened in the vision God showed me. My face was shining with the brightness of His face. God desired that I'd be more of Him and less of me and that people would see it when they look at my life. This all happened in broad daylight.

God is doing a great work in you. God will begin to reveal Himself to you and I pray that even as you are in your bedrooms that you would have a visitation by the Lord Himself, and that He would reveal His mysteries to you.

Treasures Truth

Having dreams and visions quite a bit? If that's you, you may be a Seer in the Spirit. Allow the Lord to develop you and look into training and literature about the prophetic. Also, reach out to your leadership in your local church to help you grow in your gifting.

Today I Will...

- Trust the Lord to develop my gifting.
- Pray for Him to connect me with the right people to mentor and guide me.

Let's Pray...

Heavenly Father, I thank You for developing my gifting in the area of visions. I know that this gift came from You and I ask that You hone and sharpen it in me. I thank You that through visions, I can see the abundant power, supply, and solutions that You have for the world, which are more than I can even comprehend. I ask that You would cause me to experience You on a deeper level, as my spiritual senses are awakened with visions.

In Jesus' Name,

Amen.

DEVOTION 38

Sowing Seeds

**"As long as the earth endures,
seedtime and harvest,
cold and heat,
summer and winter,
day and night
will never cease."
(Genesis 8:22)**

There will be times in your life where you sow seeds and you may reap a harvest in a completely different way. I remember just feeling led to sow $1,000 one day to a very well-known ministry. Now, two years went by after I sowed that seed, and I said to myself, "Wow, I don't recall reaping a harvest from that seed," and then the Holy Spirit began to speak. I heard Him say, *"Yes, you did reap a harvest. Your harvest is your current job and the promotion that came along with it."* At that moment, I realized that you can sow a seed and reap a harvest in a different form. I was thinking I would receive money back, which I did, but that seed caused me to receive a new job and experience. Now, the seed did cause me to receive an increase but you never know *what* God will cause you to reap when you sow good seeds.

Some of you may be thinking, "I don't have that kind of money to sow," but who says it only has to be money? A couple of years ago, my dad had a stroke and I moved back home to help my parents. There may be a lot of you doing this as well. I remember, there were weekends that I couldn't go out with friends all the time because I had decided to help my Dad on those weekends. Now, from the outside looking in, people may say that those years were not used in the right way, but I choose to look at it differently. Those years were seeds sown in the ground. To this day, my dad still says, "I'll never forget how you helped me."

When you help others, God sees it, and the Bible does say that God keeps a record of things in heaven. That sounds like good news to me! God sees the good deeds that you are doing on the earth. Those seeds can produce unlimited favor in your life, preferential treatment, and big doors to be opened that you couldn't open on your own.

"Do not be deceived: God cannot be mocked.
A man reaps what he sows.
Whoever sows to please their flesh,
from the flesh will reap destruction;
whoever sows to please the Spirit,
from the Spirit will reap eternal life.
Let us not become weary in doing good,
for at the proper time we will reap a harvest
if we do not give up.
Therefore, as we have opportunity,
let us do good to all people,
especially to those who belong
to the family of believers."
(Galatians 6:7-9)

Treasures of Truth

What seeds are you sowing today? Get into the habit of sowing good seeds. Begin to prepare for a great harvest.

Today I Will...

- Pray over every seed that I sow.
- Expect and anticipate bountiful harvests in my life as I sow good seeds.

Let's Pray...

Heavenly Father, I thank You that in blessings You will bless me and in multiplying, You will multiply my seed. Thank You for multiplying my seed as the sand on the seashore. I thank You for rebuking the devourer for my sake and not allowing Him to destroy the fruits of the ground. Thank You for tending to the seeds that I have sown in the ground, and cause them to harvest in the proper time and season. Lead me to a good ground to sow into and cause me to be a blessing.

In the Mighty Name of Jesus,

Amen.

Words Have Power!

"The tongue has the power of life and death, and those who love it will eat its fruit."
(Proverbs 18:21)

What are you saying about yourself? I remember a season of my life when I was dealing with insecurity and the fear of man and God used people who were not saved to begin to speak life over me. Every time this one guy would come by my desk, he would always say, "Hey, Big Time!" Of ourse, my response back was very modest and I would say, "No, I'm not Big Time," and he would say, "Yes you are. You're going to keep on going up and up and up." Then after he kept going on, I just accepted what he said and didn't refuse his words, and then the Holy Spirit began to speak to me right at my desk. He said, *"Even when you won't speak words of life over yourself, I will bring people around to speak life into the atmosphere over you."* I was blown away by what the Holy Spirit told me. I thought to myself, "Wow, God, you love me that much!"

There will be seasons or moments in your life where you don't feel like you have the strength to speak life into the atmosphere and I believe that is when God steps in to help out. Do you know how powerful words are? In the beginning, God spoke words to bring things into existence and they came to be. Therefore, we have the same ability to speak things into the atmosphere and watch them manifest into the natural. After the Holy Spirit spoke to me, I began to pay attention to the words that I was releasing into the atmosphere and started to speak life over myself and others on purpose. What are you saying?

Treasures of Truth

In James, we read the following about the power of the tongue:

"Likewise, the tongue is a small part of the body, but it makes great boasts. Consider what a great forest is set on fire by a small spark. The tongue also is a fire, a world of evil among the parts of the body. It corrupts the whole body, sets the whole course of one's life on fire, and is itself set on fire by hell."
(James 3:5-6)

As believers, we tend to see this Scripture in relation to gossip and how we speak about others. However, if we see it in relation to the words we speak over our lives, it gives us a better understanding of the power of life and death being in the words we speak.

Speak words of life and truth into the atmosphere!

"For, 'Whoever would love life
and see good days must keep
their tongue from evil and their
lips from deceitful speech.
They must turn from evil and do good;
they must seek peace and pursue it.
For the eyes of the Lord are on the righteous
and his ears are attentive to their prayer,
but the face of the Lord is against
those who do evil.'"
(1 Peter 3:10-12)

Today I Will...

- Speak words of life and truth over my life and into the atmosphere.
- Speak blessings and not curses over the people I encounter.

Let's Pray...

Great God, I thank You that You load me daily with benefits. As I meditate on Your Word day and night, I thank You that I am successful and prosperous. I thank You that I prosper in all things and I remain in health even as my soul prospers. As I read Your Word, Holy Spirit, I ask that You would illuminate certain Scriptures and words that I should declare over myself daily. As I renew my mind daily, constantly remind of the authority that I have in You and release words of life into the atmosphere. I speak blessings over myself now and I thank You that You have a great future prepared for me.

In Jesus' Name,
Amen.

DEVOTION 40

Levels of Pressure

"That the trial of your faith, being much more precious than of gold that perisheth, though it be tried with fire, might be found unto praise and honour and glory at the appearing of Jesus Christ: Whom having not seen, ye love; in whom, though now ye see him not, yet believing, ye rejoice with joy unspeakable and full of glory: Receiving the end of your faith, even the salvation of your souls."
(1 Peter 1:7-9)

My father would always say, "Renee, the higher you go up the ladder, the more pressure you'll have," and I have started to experience exactly what he was talking about. I have noticed the different levels of pressure that I have endured and the interesting thing is that the Lord led me right into the direction of that pressure. Look at the children of Israel. God knew there were giants already in the land, but He still led them right in their direction. I am going to be real. There will be times where you will feel like it's a lot and inundated with responsibilities, but that's where you rely on His grace.

All throughout my career, I noticed that when God opened specific doors for me in leadership roles, the pressure increased. Looking back, if I had known ahead about some of the pressure I faced, I probably would have declined those jobs. However, God knew what He was doing; He allowed the pressure to make me.

As you keep getting promoted, you'll notice that your level of responsibility will increase and most times, there will be no one to fall back on but God and yourself. When God wants you to grow and get you out of a mind frame that is somewhat childish and full of fear, He will make you face things head on. You may feel tempted to want to lean on someone or wish you had someone to fall back on, but God is allowing you to experience this discomfort and level of pressure because He is preparing you for what is ahead. This can be a preview to where God is taking you, and you need to become comfortable with the different levels of leadership and pressure that God puts you in because there are people waiting on you to pass the test. Keep going, pass the test! You can do it!

"There's more to come: We continue to shout our praise even when we're hemmed in with troubles, because we know how troubles can develop passionate patience in us, and how that patience in turn forges the tempered steel of virtue, keeping us alert for whatever God will do next. In alert expectancy such as this, we're never left feeling shortchanged. Quite the contrary—we can't round up enough containers to hold everything God generously pours into our lives through the Holy Spirit!"
(Romans 5:3-5, MSG)

Treasures of Truth

This is a journey, led by the Holy Spirit and planned by God. As you grow, He will determine the levels of pressure and responsibility. He will also strengthen you to bear it.

**"But those who wait on the Lord
Shall renew *their* strength;
They shall mount up with wings like eagles,
They shall run and not be weary,
They shall walk and not faint."
(Isaiah 40:31, NKJV)**

Today I Will...

- Trust the Lord's plan that He has for my life.
- Remember that He is right there with me and is allowing this season to refine me.
- Allow patience to have its perfect work in me.

Let's Pray...

Heavenly Father, I thank You that You are the potter and I am the clay. I thank You for refining me and using my life to bring glory to Your name. Even when the pressure feels great, I thank You that I will endure hardness as a good soldier. I ask that You give me overcoming grace to remain under the pressure. Even when I am hard pressed on every side, I am not abandoned. I may feel perplexed at times, but I am never in despair and struck down, and never destroyed.

In Jesus' Name,

Amen.

FINAL THOUGHTS

In this world's system, it seems like there is no righteousness and the world wants you to conform to their lifestyle and way of doing things. However, God has a Remnant that will resist the thought patterns of this world and will stand up for righteousness in the earth. As part of God's Remnant, there are mandates, calls, assignments, Kingdom responsibilities, and platforms that God has lined up for you to fulfill. God has anointed you for the call that He has on your life. As you are on your journey, like David, God is preparing you for your appointed time, when you step into that platform, ministry, assignment, and role.

Something that God has been instilling in me during my process now is integrity. I remember Him saying, *"Renee, I am big on integrity, and when I give you a platform and certain things, you have to make sure to take good care of it and to steward it well."* He went on to say how serious it was and it shook me up a bit because when God elevates you and places you in authority, it's serious business! It's His work. At that moment, when God was speaking to me, I felt like I was growing in Him. In your journey with the Lord, you'll notice that He'll begin to talk to you differently. I felt that God began to trust me and showed me that I was no longer a babe in Christ. I felt like Paul when he said, "When I was a child, I thought like a child, but when I became a man, I put away childish things." I began to embrace and accept this charge and level of responsibility that the Lord had given me.

An important key along the journey is to have a strong sense of your identity in Christ. For many years, because of the bullying I experienced at a young age, I struggled with comparison and felt threatened by others, which was and is Satan's plan. He tries to plant this self-hate and self-rejection in girls and boys at very young ages to try to steal their identities and cause them to lose their uniqueness and become like everyone else.

However, to those of you reading this right now, you are not like everyone else and you will never be! God has called you to be set apart, to be who He created you to be. You are God's Remnant! You are kings on Earth, a peculiar people, a royal priesthood, and the salt and light of the world. You are royalty and royalty stands out. You have your own flavor and it has KINGDOM written all over it! We are here to change the world!

"'You are the light of the world. A city that is set on a hill cannot be hidden. Nor do they light a lamp and put it under a basket, but on a lampstand, and it gives light to all who are in the house. Let your light so shine before men, that they may see your good works and glorify your Father in heaven.'"
(Matthew 5:14-16, NKJV)

ACKNOWLEDGMENTS & THANKS

I would first like to thank God for giving me the mandate and assignment to write this book. I thank You, Lord, for entrusting me with sharing Your message and Your Words to Your people. I ask that this book brings glory to You and You are pleased with the work. I love You with all my heart.

To my dear family — Dixie, Phillip, Jamal, Kisha, Brandon, and Jael. Thank you so much for supporting me with this project. I appreciate the time you've invested by listening to me cite my manuscript several times and helping me with Scriptures. Thank you for helping to bring this vision to life. I love you!

Also, thank you to Pastor Kisia Coleman, editor Noleen Arendse, and the entire KishKnows Self-Publishing Company staff. I am truly appreciative of all your contributions to this book's existence and helping me so much throughout this process. I appreciate the creative touch on the designs and thank you for helping me birth this book and vision from the Lord.

Also, to my friends and family, (aunts, uncles, and cousins) thank you for the love and support with this book. May God bless you!

ABOUT THE AUTHOR

Renee Gardner is a business professional. She loves to empower young people to discover their God-given purpose. Renee is a graduate of Oral Roberts University (ORU) where she earned a bachelor's degree in Business Management in 2007, as well as a Master of Business Administration in 2009. She attended Revival Fellowship Church and sat under the leadership of Pastor W.W. Koonce and Pastors Troy and Renay Dorsey. Her extensive training at Revival Fellowship Church and ORU afforded her the opportunity to glean from great teaching, which included training in the prophetic, healing, and signs and wonders. Renee resides in Newark, Delaware and is currently working on releasing more publications and God-ordained projects.

CONTACT THE AUTHOR

I would love to hear from my readers, so please connect with me. Subscribe to my website via www. ReneeGardnerMinistries.com

I am also on social media. Add me on Facebook at Renee Michelle or Like my ministry page Renee Gardner Ministries, and Follow me on Instagram: @Renee_Michelle7